Damn Right
I've Got The Blues

Buddy Guy and the Blues Roots
of Rock-and-Roll

◆

Donald E. Wilcock
with Buddy Guy

Rick Siciliano
Principal Photographer

Woodford Press

San Francisco

Woodford Press

(A division of Woodford Publishing, Inc.)
660 Market Street, Suite 206
San Francisco, California 94104

Publisher/Creative Director: Laurence J. Hyman
Editor: Jon Rochmis
Art Director: Jim Santore
Book Design: Todd Everett
Marketing/Distribution: David Lilienstein
Editorial Assistants: Kate Hanley, Molly Stadum

PHOTOGRAPHS

Rick Siciliano (principal photographer): Pages 3, 4, 6-bottom, 7-bottom, 8, 11-17, 20-25, 37, 39-bottom, 41, 43, 47-51, 55, 58, 64, 66, 67, 70, 72, 74-76, 79, 80, 83, 87, 89, 91, 94, 95, 97, 101, 105, 108, 111, 114-120, 122, 123, 125, 131, 132, 135, 137, 138-139, 141, 144-147, back cover-middle, bottom.

Stephen Green: Pages ii, 7, 9, 57, 77, 78, 79-top, 82, 98, 99, 110, back cover-top.

Annie Mae Guy: Pages 35, 40.

Jack Vartoogian: Front Cover, Pages 5, 106.

Stephen Orlick: Page vi.

Mike Vernon: Pages 29, 30, 31, 42, 45, 63, 65.

Marty Salzman: Pages 6-top, 84, 113.

Susan Antone Archives: Pages 32, 36, 112, 124, 126.

Mark PoKempner: Pages 52-53, 102-103, 109, 142-143.

Stephen LaVere: Pages 54, 73.

Don Bronstein: Pages 60-61 (courtesy Jim O'Neal collection).

Jim O'Neal: Pages 60-61, 92.

Stuart Brinin: Page 129.

David Booth: Page 39.

Rob Dicker: Page 86.

Peter Jordan: Page 96.

ISBN: 0-94267-13-X
Library of Congress Card Catalog Number: 91-075201

First printing September 1993
Printed in the USA

Contents

Preface

I t has been a music critic's dream to work with Buddy Guy on the story of his musical career, and none of this would have happened without an assist from my fellow critic, Michael Hochanadel. When Buddy told Michael during a 1988 interview that he was looking for some help on his authorized biography, Michael recommended me. For that I am eternally grateful.

I'd like to thank all the musicians who contributed to this project. The information contained here was obtained almost exclusively through one-on-one interviews with people eager to go on record about the impact Buddy has had on their lives. Some, Stevie Ray Vaughan and Willie Dixon in particular, are no longer with us. Others, such as Eric Clapton, Ron Wood, Bill Wyman, Carlos Santana and Jeff Beck, continue to spread the word that Buddy Guy is a true inspiration. Their willingness to be interviewed makes this a living commentary on an artist they love.

This book is not a biography in the traditional sense. It is more of an oral history, one that explores the immense impact Buddy Guy has had on the seminal guitar superstars, as well as on Rock-and-Roll's second and third generations. But it contradicts the purist blues thesis that rock merely robs from blues and gives nothing in return. Buddy Guy owes a share of his success to the rock stars who credit his influence. Unlike many blues musicians of his generation,

Buddy is not at all bitter towards and in fact considers himself friends with younger, much more financially successful rock stars who borrowed liberally from his music.

Sometimes, my emotions carried me away from the facts. I could always count on Woodford Press publisher Laurence J. Hyman and editor Jon Rochmis to pull me back to reality and put this manuscript into perspective. I am indebted to them for countless hours of discussion and help as this book took form over the past two years. Kate Hanley, Leah Katz and David Lilienstein also were of tremendous editorial assistance.

Most of the photographs were taken by my good friend, Rick Siciliano. We would stop at nothing to get the story and that critical photograph, from sharing a Jack-and-Ginger with Jack Bruce in the basement bar of the Royal Albert Hall, to capturing Buddy's mood as he returned to the plantation where he was born.

Finally, I'd like to thank Michele Green and my children, David and Michael, for putting up with the long hours and my moodiness while producing this manuscript. Without their encouragement, I never would have seen this through.

Donald E. Wilcock
Scotia, N.Y.
May 1993

Foreword

I always had fantasies about being a Chicago bluesman, driving around in a Cadillac and living the life. Now I know how difficult it is just to be a musician, let alone support that kind of lifestyle. Now I'd just like to trade places with Buddy for his musicianship, the strength of his hands and his unending enthusiasm for the music.

Buddy is the last generation of the true blues musicians as we know them. He knows the language and speaks it as I imagine he always did. He's the last one-of-a-kind, he-man of the blues, a muscleman of the guitar heroes.

When Buddy played the Marquee Club in London in 1965, I saw an amplified bluesman for the first time. He was the epitome of it all, and he really changed the course of Rock-and-Roll and blues. He gave us something to strive for—the way he dressed, the way he moved, the way he expressed himself. He's still doing it, but he was established as someone to copy many, many years ago.

It's always a blast to see Buddy play live. He comes through the way he is, playing with his teeth, on the floor, throwing his guitar around. A lot of people can't get away with that, but he can because he not only has the nerve but he can entertain and make good music too.

He's one of the few you can trust to get up and play whatever he feels and have it still be great. He has that power. He's a band on his own. When Buddy tells his band to shut up and get out of the way, they stop. It takes self-confidence and awareness. You've got to be a man to pull that off, believe me.

It's a very comfortable and exalted feeling to be around him. I still get a lift from him. If I'm around Buddy I'll play like him just to wind him up. He knows I can do it, and it's all in fun.

Buddy Guy is the best. You can't say more than that. He is a consummate blues musician. And he's probably the last of that generation. He's living history.

Eric Clapton
London, 1991

1

The Roots Of Rock

"All of a sudden, somebody like Stevie Ray Vaughan would go and make a record and liven blues back up again. Then everybody would come back to me like I was a piece of meat that had been frozen in the refrigerator for a while, pull me out, and say, 'It's still good.'"

—Buddy Guy

Rock-and-Roll evolved as a hybrid of folk, country, Rhythm-and-Blues and blues. But somewhere between the birth of Rock-and-Roll and its rebirth in the mid-1960s—a renaissance influenced by the "British Invasion"—the link between rock and blues became frayed, the result of the forces of marketing style over artistic substance.

The music marketers, as always zeroing in on popular music's teen appeal, looked for faces and personalities with which young people could identify. Performers such as Neil Sedaka, Frankie Avalon and Fabian drew more inspiration from the emerging teen culture they were helping to define than they did from the energy and emotions of the blues.

Buddy Guy was part of the same era that produced Chuck Berry, Bo Diddley, Little Richard and Fats Domino, all of whom kept an open line between the development of their music and the simultaneous evolution of blues from a rural acoustic form to an urban electric sound. They were one generation younger than Muddy Waters, B.B. King and Howlin' Wolf, the accepted patriarchs of postwar urban electric blues. Their roots, in turn, were tied to the generation of the original blues musicians who played on back porches and in roadside taverns.

Perhaps more than anyone else, Buddy was the link that connected the eras. Muddy Waters fed a penniless Buddy Guy. Buddy's first theater appearance was as the opening act for B.B. King in Chicago. He was on the same label as Howlin' Wolf, appeared on recordings with Sonny Boy Williamson and was the guitarist on Koko Taylor's classic blues hit "Wang Dang Doodle." His appearances at festivals and rock concerts in 1967 prepared audiences for Jimi Hendrix, a black, blues-based rocker who would take the guitar into psychedelic no-man's-land, previously explored by Guy in concert, but not on record.

Because he was completely self-taught—and inexplicably burdened by an insecure fear that he would never be quite as good as the masters—Buddy felt his approach had to be different. He wanted to play with the finesse of B.B. King and the flamboyance of Guitar Slim, a wild, maverick, yet obscure Rhythm-and-Blues musician known for his loud guitar playing and outrageous stage show.

By combining those two influences, Buddy Guy hoped he would be accepted among his idols in Chicago. All he wanted was just to play in the same clubs they did. He was oblivious to the fact he was creating a unique sound.

Buddy's attempts to increase his volume were greeted with thrilled response and whiskey bottle prizes at Sunday afternoon cutting contests in Chicago blues bars. But in the recording studio, his pyrotechnics were dismissed as "noise" by Leonard Chess of Chess Records.

Buddy Guy was, and is, an innovator in a style of music that rewards innovation far less than it reveres tradition.

The independent labels that were recording blues when Buddy migrated from rural Louisiana to Chicago were marketing to some of the same people Buddy had just left on the Southern plantations. Sales were minuscule by pop standards, and there was very little room to experiment with new sounds. It wasn't until 1965 that an entire electric blues bar band was recorded the way it performed in the South and West Side Chicago clubs. That first recording, *Hoodoo Man Blues* by the Junior Wells Blues Band, included an appearance by "Friendly Chap," Buddy Guy.

Still, Buddy Guy sparked the imagination of an entire generation of young musicians frustrated by the music industry's sanitized pop music. One chief example: He was using feedback as an integral element of his guitar playing as early as 1958, nine years before Jimi Hendrix "revolutionized" the rock world with his psychedelic distortions.

Hendrix had been listening to Buddy Guy.

By the time Buddy was discovered by his future manager, Dick Waterman, Hendrix had followed up on Buddy's dramatic impact on the British scene and stolen his thunder.

The burgeoning folk market also initially discounted urban blues. Among others, Mississippi John Hurt and Big Bill Broonzy, with their rural tra-

Buddy has been known to wander in the unlikeliest of places during his extended guitar solos.

Eric Clapton jams with Buddy at the Checkerboard, 1987.

ditions, were considered folk, as opposed to the young electric artists such as Otis Rush, Magic Sam, Earl Hooker and Buddy Guy.

Blues again strongly influenced popular music beginning around 1962. British teenagers, including Eric Clapton, Jeff Beck, Bill Wyman and Eric Burdon, were exploring the imported works of electric blues musicians appearing on the Chess label—most notably Chuck Berry and Muddy Waters. Also, the American folk movement plugged in electrically and abandoned its elitist attitude toward original material, opening the door for Chicago blues to fit under this expanded umbrella. Around the same time, white Chicago students began to discover electric blues as an exciting alternative to bar band

Buddy, Bo Diddley and Lou Reed at the Inter-national Rock Awards *rehearsal, 1990.*

*British blues pioneer
John Mayall appeared
on* Feels Like Rain.

Rock-and-Roll. Performers such as Muddy Waters and Buddy Guy began to share the stage with white blues bands, among them the Paul Butterfield Blues Band at Uncle John's on the mostly white North Side.

While Butterfield, the Steve Miller Band, the Blues Project and Tom Rush were turning on white, college-student folk and rock fans to electric blues in the United States, the British rock guitarists were informing their countrymen and Americans alike about a living blues heritage that until then had been largely ignored. If British rock guitarists who appreciated their music's heritage had not spoken out about his importance, Buddy Guy might still be playing Louisiana roadhouses or not playing at all.

The failure of Chess, Vanguard and subsequent small record labels to capture the essence of the live Buddy Guy performance style only increased the mystery and intrigue surrounding his growing legend. Clapton may be "God" to his fans, yet to Clapton, there are none better than Buddy Guy. Clapton's fans could have no idea of what Buddy was all about by listening to Buddy's records, but those who saw him play live knew differently.

JIMMIE VAUGHAN: *"Somebody told me they saw Buddy Guy play one time around 1968 when he had that live recording from San Francisco with the horn section. They said he was playing solo and all this wild stuff. He put his guitar down and was singing. One of the strings started feeding back. O-o-o-o-o-o. He pulled out his handkerchief, threw it over his shoulder. It landed on the strings and stopped the guitar. He didn't even look back. That's the kind of stuff guitar players hear about Buddy Guy. This magic stuff. How did he do that?"*

Jimmie Vaughan

Unfortunately, the true essence of Buddy Guy's sound would not be recorded, distributed and accepted by a mass audience until well into his

*Jerry Portnoy and
Albert Collins with
Buddy during 1991
Royal Albert Hall show.*

career. Having been discounted first in the 1950s by Chess and then in the 1960s by record executives who had already exploited musicians he had influenced, Buddy had long since become disgusted with the politics and inadequate support of small labels. A major-label deal always seemed to be just around the corner, and there it always remained. It wasn't until 1990 that the long-awaited deal came through and the world finally got to hear Buddy Guy as a musical force quite separate from his Chicago blues mentors. That album, after which this book is named, rightfully earned Buddy a Grammy Award.

One could argue forever whether the lines common to Buddy, Eric Clapton and Stevie Ray Vaughan were originally influenced by Buddy's own early playing. Some may be lured to Buddy's playing because they hear a refrain from Cream's "Sunshine of Your Love," or they may think Buddy is copying Stevie Ray Vaughan when he rages through his own "Mary Had A Little Lamb," which in fact was a cover made popular by Vaughan. Buddy is not afraid to admit he gets inspiration back from them, too, as heard on "Rememberin' Stevie" from his *Damn Right, I've Got the Blues* album.

Buddy readily admits he thought several times of giving up the life of a professional guitarist, so deep was his frustration and so frequent were his disappointments. Combined with his lifelong stage fright and given his steadfast refusal to acknowledge his musical virtuosity—Buddy consistently insists there are dozens of blues guitarists more talented than he—it is remarkable that he didn't quit. That he continues to play despite these insecurities, yet with the same fire he brought to Chicago's 708 Club more than 35 years ago, is testament to his passionate love for the guitar and the blues and his intense desire to please his audience.

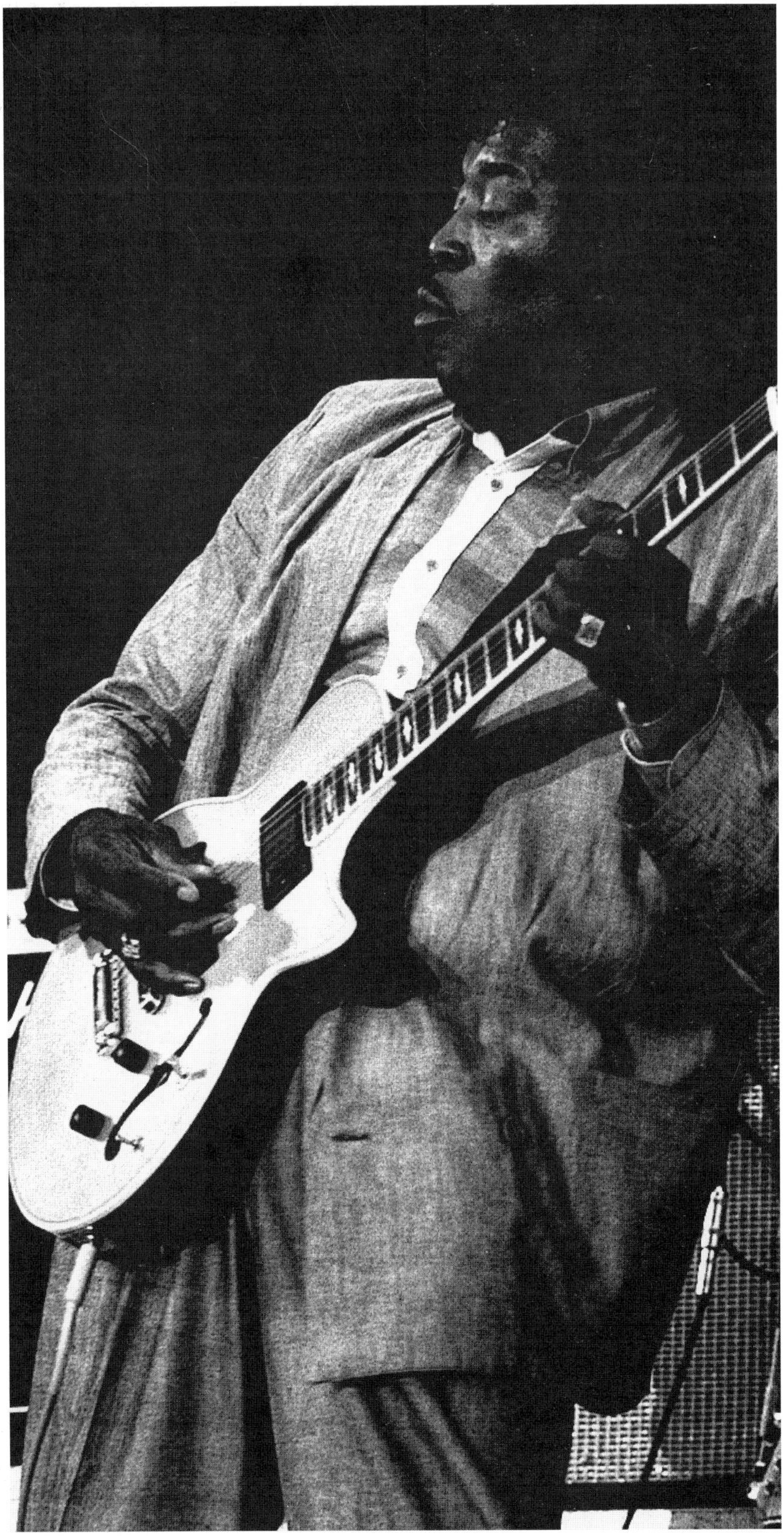

BUDDY GUY: *"Earl Hooker, Matt Murphy, Magic Sam, Freddy King, Luther Allison—these guys were playing so much guitar, something told me, 'Don't even take your guitar out of the case.'*

"But then something would tell me, 'Take it out of the case, hook it behind your back or put it behind your head. Just do anything to make somebody pay attention to you.' I was doing something different. And in the meantime, I was going through the process of learning, too. Sure, I can play. But there's better and best. These guys were there by the millions in Chicago. I would walk up and they'd say, 'Who are you?'

"'I'm a guitar player, man.'

"And you'd give them that guitar and say, 'Oh, shit. Why do I spend all my time? Who the hell is this?' That's just how the guitar player was in Chicago in 1957-58. They didn't give a shit about me. I was just somebody who came there from Louisiana, but I had a long, 150-foot cord and I was sticking my guitar up in the roof and walking away and leaving it and laying it on the ground with the G-string open. And they was saying, 'What the hell is he doing?'

"I'd say, 'I'm doing something you guys ain't.'"

2 Sharecropping Blues

"Every time my mama would walk into church, she'd start crying. This is the thing I feel when I play—the Baptist coming out of me, 'cause I seen it done a lot of times in the Baptist church. People get up, and they just get to shakin', and they scream out loud. They get into that shoutin' thing and bringing it from inside 'til my chill runs out my eyes. They say that's the spirit coming out of you."

—Buddy Guy

I t wasn't that sharecropping was a terrible life as much as it was tedious and unending. Six days a week, sunup to sunset, the routine never changed. Neither, usually, did the economic status of those who tended land owned by other, richer families. Half of everything Sam and Isabell Guy made off their patch of land in Lettsworth, Louisiana, went to the Fetudia family. The Guys never starved, but they never seemed to make any money, either. In the spring, the Fetudias might front a $20 allowance that had to be paid back before any earnings were tendered. In a year of poor crops, the family might end up owing more than it earned, the debt carried over into the next year.

BUDDY GUY: *"Farming was like throwing the dice on the table at Vegas. You know you're not going to beat 'em."*

The town of Lettsworth, 50 miles north of Baton Rouge on Route 1, was little more than a general store at the side of a road that stretched from horizon to horizon. The flat land was protected from the Mississippi River by an endless, sloping, man-made mound of grass. A person could walk the levee from Lettsworth to Bachelor and, if so inclined, all the way south to Baton Rouge. In the spring when the river bulged against the banks, workers in bulldozers would build up the dirt to hold back the currents that threatened to bleed through the fields. Sometimes, though, as in the devastating floods

Buddy grew up near this house in Lettsworth.

during the summer of 1993, nature proved too powerful even against man's strongest efforts.

In the middle of a field at the edge of the levee, in a weathered matchbox that was their home, George "Buddy" Guy lived with his parents, his younger brothers Sam and Philip, and his older sisters Annie Mae and Fanny. Isabell Guy worked in the big house, cooking for the plantation owners. Sam, the father, tended the cotton crop, labor that provided the source not only of his immense strength which belied his small stature, but helped assure his family's survival as well.

Annie Mae

ANNIE MAE: *"Dad was a good father, but he wasn't really a provider. A lot of things he could not do. But what he could do, he did well. He worked on the railroad for a while. He would cut timber, stuff like that. But he never really was a farmer. My dad never did seem to make good crops."*

Everyone in the family was expected to help out. When he wasn't in school, Buddy would follow a mule behind a plow, or pick cotton.

BUDDY GUY: *"My parents used to say, 'We don't want you to be like us. We want you to get as much education as you can and get away from here. There's no future here.' They had smiles on their faces when they said that as if to say, 'We did this for you.'"*

Weekends provided the only diversions from this otherwise repetitive existence. On Saturday mornings, Buddy was allowed to pick cotton, sell it, and keep all the money as profit. On a good day, he'd pick 100 pounds and make $2.50. Then he'd go to the store, buy a Nehi Orange and a bag of peanuts. He'd drop the peanuts into the soda bottle, wait until they swelled up, then eat them. Lunch.

SAM GUY (BUDDY'S BROTHER): *"I used to pick 300-400 pounds of cotton a day. We'd pick it all and take a sack, put it across a horse, take it home and weigh it. We'd be out there about 5 or 6 in the morning, stay until 11 or 12. If you didn't see your shadow, you knew it was noon. We'd come on in, take a rest and maybe mama'd cook something. Then we'd go back to work until sunset."*

By the setting sun, Buddy would play baseball with his brothers and cousins. Their ball was a can, a piece of equipment as valuable as a real ball. If the can was hit over the levee, Buddy would try to hear where it landed in the high weeds, then retrieve it. But just as often as play baseball, Buddy would sit on a wood pile with a button and a piece of string, threading the button and stretching the string between his fingers, listening to the button sing as it swirled on the string up and down like a yo-yo. Resonating in the stillness of the moist Southern air, every sound seemed richer.

On Sunday mornings, the Guys went to church.

FANNY: *"They were good times. Good times. There was no piano playing, no choir. Everyone just sang together, clapping and stomping their feet to the wooden floors."*

Christmas was different too, the only special day the Guys celebrated.

BUDDY GUY: *"Christmas was the only big holiday we had in the country. Easter Sunday was fine. You'd go to church. Then it was back to work. The Fourth of July we knew nothing about. Thanksgiving was just another Thursday. No turkey. You just worked. But Christmas was different. We went to the store for a barrel of flour, baking powder and salt. The rest of the stuff we had in the yard. We'd get a pig and cut the pig's throat. The greens came from the garden. The cake mama put in the*

Buddy and Sam Guy visit family grave site in Lettsworth, 1991.

Buddy used to hang out at the Rock Shop, where proprietor Buddy Stewart first suggested a move to Chicago.

wood stove. I'd take the horse and wagon to get wood. We'd make a fire in the stove where she did the baking. She'd make this coconut cake. She knew how to do coconut so it would come out in these little strings like you'd buy. You'd look at this cake, and it was beautiful and white. She would put whatever she'd put between it and say, 'You can't eat at it. It's gotta set three or four days so it could soak down in the cake.' I'd be there like a rat. She'd say, 'Why don't you go play?' I'd say, 'I'm not going nowhere!' As soon as she'd finish cooking I'd be there.

"Christmas morning, everybody had a big gallon of wine and a case of beer. They'd drink it up in my parents' house and go on to my uncle's house. At night, they went to this white guy's country joint and put nickels in the jukebox to play Muddy Waters and John Lee Hooker."

Buddy would sit in the corner of the juke joint while Sam and Isabell danced, sang and laughed, partying into the night. Buddy's favorite time was when Henry Smith—"Coot" for short—would edge tentatively toward the dance floor clutching his beat-up guitar in one hand and a bottle of whiskey in the other.

Coot was the only man on the plantation who played music. Most of the time, he would hang out down by the big boats on Three Rivers, but on Christmas, he'd have a few drinks and summon enough courage to play for the celebration. Buddy would sneak forward, slip into a chair and listen intently to Coot's fumbling attempt to pluck music from his strings. Annie Mae remembered Coot as "a short man who played repetitious, fumbling guitar and would act drunk to cover up that he couldn't play. He only knew 'Boogie Chillen.'"

BUDDY GUY: *"When I was seven or eight, they'd try to get me to go to bed. They'd look around, and I'd be there in the doorway with my clothes on. I'd be standing up with my hands between my legs shyly. I wasn't leaving if there was a guitar stringer around. That was the only music."*

Finally, asleep in front of Coot, Buddy would be scooped up by his father and carried home.

A world beyond the plantation was brought to Buddy through the family's battery-operated radio. When it was raining, the radio would crackle and scratch, but sometimes at night it could pick up stations that played country music, jazz and blues.

BUDDY GUY: *"The deejays would put on a spiritual record, and then a John Lee Hooker, then a Hank Williams, and I wouldn't turn my radio off. It was always a surprise, and I loved it all. I didn't want the station just to play the blues. At the same time, Muddy Waters, Walter and the Wolf, and John Lee Hooker, those people were the music to listen to. There wasn't as many fans as there is now. It was predominantly black music being played to a black audience.*

"When Elvis came out with 'All Shook Up,' I was singing it just like I was 'Hoochie Coochie Man.' It made no difference. I didn't care what color a person

Annie Mae with one of Buddy's earliest guitars.

Lunch with Sam at
Annie Mae's home.

*was. Let other people worry about that. I just loved good music, man. I didn't give
a damn who played it."*

When his folks picked up an old windup record player and began buying blues records, Buddy started to ignore his playmates to listen to the music.

The exciting, down-home sounds of Muddy Waters, Howlin' Wolf,
Arthur Crudup, Lonnie Johnson and Little Walter hypnotized Buddy. He'd sit
by the hour imagining what it would be like to play in front of a big audience.

BUDDY GUY: *"On a rainy day, I would lie in front of the radio and fall asleep
listening to Muddy Waters or Howlin' Wolf. I would dream that was me. All these
people would be looking at me, and I was standing there playing. And I wasn't shy.
I'd wake up and say, 'Wow, that was me.' Then I'd stop and say, 'No, that wasn't
close. You can't do that in front of nobody.'"*

Buddy was becoming obsessed with the guitar. He'd pick up a broom
and pretend to be playing Lightnin' Hopkins. He'd string rubber bands
between two nails he drove into the wall and pluck them endlessly, absorbed
in the twang. He'd even get more inventive, taking individual strands of
screen wire—which Buddy's parents had nailed to the windows to keep the
mosquitoes out—and connect them to paint cans to make rudimentary guitars. There was no one to teach Buddy how to play it; he would later shrug
and say his ability was a gift from God.

The Carriage House was once named Sitman's, the site of Buddy's first live appearance.

BUDDY GUY: *"The mosquitoes were big enough in Louisiana to pick you up and carry you out of the room. But I didn't give a damn as long as I had those strings. No sooner had they fixed the screens than the mosquitoes would be biting again. My parents would look at the window and there was nothing hanging down. I'd break 'em. Every time, my dad would get 'em and tie 'em back around.*

"Lightnin' Slim's electric guitar was the first I'd ever seen. I didn't know what it was. He came out to the front porch of this storefront. He had a pickup on an acoustic. He plugged that thing in and started playing 'Boogie Chillen.' That little amplifier was a little bigger than a transistor radio. I didn't know a guitar could sound like that."

Drinking-age limitations did not exist in Louisiana, and when Buddy reached adolescence, his father would sometimes take him to the roadhouses that dotted the highways snaking out of Baton Rouge. Like a beacon to moths, these nondescript shacks would attract motorists from the road into the bar, where some of the same people Buddy had heard on the radio were performing live.

Sometimes, Buddy and his friends would buy a quart of beer for 45 cents and sneak behind a roadhouse for a drink. His father didn't object to his drinking, although Isabell disapproved.

BUDDY GUY: *"He was keeping us out late at night. Mama would say, 'Now, don't keep those boys out past midnight.' Daddy'd say, 'Oh mama, you know I ain't gonna keep them out that long.' So, he'd bring us in about 4:30 or quarter to 5. And we wouldn't let her put on the light. So he'd tell us to crawl. And she had this stick. We'd be crawlin', and she'd say, 'What time is it?'*

"'Oh mama, it's early.'

"As soon as he said that, the rooster would crow. And she'd start hitting with this stick, man. Whoop, whoop, whoop."

Louisiana schools were racially segregated in the 1940s and 1950s. The Guy children went to a one-room school in a church down the road from their home, but the nearest high school was in Baton Rouge. Annie Mae had already made the move, vowing to escape the sharecropping life, and Buddy went to live with Annie Mae in 1950 to attend high school. Soon after Buddy moved, however, Isabell suffered a crippling stroke. Although she was still able to prepare meals and attend church, Isabell had lost the ability to speak clearly and could get around only with the help of a walker. Her poor health, coupled with the lure of playing and listening to the blues, compelled Buddy to give up his high school education after just one year to help support the family by working full time at odd jobs. His mother's illness affected him greatly; watching her slow, painful deterioration infused in him the willingness and means to survive. She died in 1968, when Buddy was 32. Buddy's father died one year earlier.

BUDDY GUY: *"I believe what's for me I'm gonna get. What isn't for me I'm not gonna get. I been without something so long that being without something don't bother me no more. I was born and raised with nothing. My mother taught me how to fix chicken to feed more than two people. A lot of people know how to give one leg to this guy and one leg to that, one wing to another and that. That's four people. Then you split the breasts. That's six. My mother taught me how to fix the chicken to feed 15—what you call stretching it. You don't give it away fried. You just take it and smother it and put gravy on it."*

3 Louisiana Roadhouse Blues

"I loved the guitar so much. It was more important to me than anything. I just wanted to be a blues guitar player. I didn't care if I was paid anything or not, because then, when it came to the point where you could get paid at it, I got to feeling very religious about it."

—Buddy Guy

In Baton Rouge clubs, Buddy could see Little Walter, Odie Payne and Luther Allison. Then on Monday night, the scene shifted to the Temple Roof Garden, a 300-seat hall on the second floor of the Masonic Temple, where the bigger acts performed: Bobby Bland, B.B. King and Guitar Slim.

It was Eddie "Guitar Slim" Jones who seized Buddy's attention. Guitar Slim was the hottest ticket on the Southern chitlins circuit after scoring the No. 1 Rhythm-and-Blues hit of 1954 with "The Things (That) I Used to Do." The story behind the song was that a devil and an angel had both come to Slim in a dream, and each offered him lyrics and a tune. He chose the devil's song, and it topped the charts for six consecutive weeks.

"The Things (That) I Used to Do" was recorded in one marathon all-night session, produced by a young Ray Charles—who also played piano on the cut. Slim turned the bass all the way down and the treble all the way up on his guitar and jammed it through a public address system—never an amplifier—at top volume, yielding a weird, crude, tinny sound.

*Guitar Slim once
appeared at the
Masonic Temple with
a young Buddy Guy
in attendance.*

His live act, and the way he dressed for it, was equally distinct and sensational, especially within the context that just about every other blues guitarist in those days played while sitting down. Thunderbird Davis, who toured with Slim in 1957, said everything was planned out in painstaking detail.

THUNDERBIRD DAVIS: *"Slim's dressing room would look like a paint shop with all his hair spray colors. He had a color for every suit. If he put on a white suit and white shoes, he'd have white hair. If he had on a loud blue suit, his hair would be bright blue."*

Slim's backup band, led by Lloyd Lambert, would play for about 15 minutes before a voice broke over the P.A. system: "Ladies and gentlemen, Mr. Guitar Slim." Instead of somebody walking on stage, a loud guitar solo sprang to life, the front door burst open, and a huge man stormed through. On his shoulders, piggy-back style—head to toe in flaming red or metallic blue or ghostly white—sat Guitar Slim. Three hundred fifty feet of guitar cord—attached to a beat-up Stratocaster with its back removed and fishing line instead of a guitar strap—trailed behind him as he made his way through the crowd. After making his rounds through the audience, Slim jumped from the shoulders of his valet, Jimmy Cole, and played in the middle of the dance floor, dropping down into a split and springing right back up. Eventually, he'd make his way to the stage and climb up into the rafters to hang by his knees while he played. Sometimes he'd cut himself by banging into something too hard, but it'd be hard to notice the blood if he were wearing his red suit. Besides, he'd never miss a beat, playing right along.

"The Things (That) I Used to Do" was Slim's ticket for the next five years, his life consumed by playing guitar, womanizing and drinking until his death in 1959 at age 33. "I live three days to y'all's one," Slim liked to say. "The world don't owe me a thing when I'm gone."

BUDDY GUY: *"When I saw him . . . I'd made up my mind. I wanted to play like B.B. but act like Guitar Slim."*

Buddy's father had bought him his first play guitar back in Lettsworth after watching his son create his own makeshift instruments.

BUDDY GUY: *"I remember him talking to one of his friends one day, and I was plucking strings. 'Boy, get away from here,' he said. 'Don't you see me talking?' The guy looked at him and said, 'No, don't run him away. That guy is going to be a great guitar player.' Then he looked at me and said, 'That's all right. Go ahead.'"*

After Buddy had moved to Baton Rouge, an uncle on his father's side, Mitchell Young, bought him his first real guitar. It cost $52.50. Buddy was never able to find him to pay him back.

Buddy would play whenever he could, often on the porch of a storefront or his sister's house, plugging a pickup into his acoustic guitar and feeding it through an amplifier the size of a transistor radio.

BUDDY GUY: *"A couple of close friends in school knew I could play. They found this big guy, Big Poppa, and told him, 'Look, we know this guy can play.' Big Poppa was looking for a guitar player, and he'd heard me at a gas station. I had just played the hell out of Jimmy Reed. He wanted someone who could play harmony."*

Buddy worked at this service station in Baton Rouge in the late 1950s.

"Big Poppa" John Tilley was willing to give a talented young unknown a chance to play with him. The next thing Buddy knew, he was on stage at a place called Sitman's, playing background for Tilley's band on the Midnighters' hit, "Work With Me, Annie."

The experience was nothing like his daydreams. The bar patrons weren't interested in a scared, young guitarist. All the faces looked ugly to him. He wanted to bolt, but instead turned his back to the crowd and played. Big Poppa fired him on the spot.

But Tilley still saw something in Buddy, a spark that prompted him to give the young musician another chance.

BUDDY GUY: *"The night of the [second] gig, again at Sitman's, a friend of mine, Raymond Brown, came and gave me some Dr. Tichenor's antiseptic mixed with some wine, and said, 'You're gonna get this job back.' They called me up, and I started singing 'Work With Me, Annie.' I guess there were about 60 people in there."*

Bolstered by the liquor, Buddy picked a young woman out of the crowd and sang to her. He watched her face light up, and that's all it took. The energy returned and Buddy let loose, focusing all those daydreams of youth into that one performance. Sitman's rocked, the crowd riveted by his delivery. Buddy quickly realized that a slug of "medicine" was a small price to pay for that kind of crowd response.

Buddy visits with a childhood friend at one of the roadhouses where he used to play.

The Rock House is halfway between Lettsworth and Baton Rouge.

Soon, Buddy was ripping up the roadhouses with Big Poppa, playing in clubs called the Three-Way Lounge, Rockin' Lucky and the Lakeland Lodge Hall, always accompanied by the two things that gave him comfort: his guitar and his "medicine."

BUDDY GUY: *"Every other week, we'd go to these different places to play. Big Poppa had an Oldsmobile. He was huge, and his wife wouldn't let him go anywhere by himself. She'd look at my older sister and tell her she couldn't go. My sister would say OK, and then wait until me, the drummer and the other guitar player sat in the back seat. Then she'd jump in and lie across us. Big Poppa wouldn't do noth-in' but drive off with us, and we'd have her lying across our laps. Big Poppa was so big nobody could get in front but him and his wife. Plus, we had all the stuff in the trunk of the car. The amplifier, guitar and drums would all fit in the trunk of that Oldsmobile 98."*

Harp player Raful Neal had a rival band, and as word got back to him about this new guitarist, he decided to see for himself.

RAFUL NEAL: *"The first time I saw him was up at Joe Bradley's Dew Drop Inn. And he was bad. He was bad! Playing out his soul. I had never seen a guy around here in Louisiana play like he did. He could play a piano boogie on guitar like nobody else. He was just a new sound in Baton Rouge."*

The next time Raful saw Big Poppa, Buddy had been replaced.

RAFUL NEAL: *"Big Poppa got a guitar player called Joe from Appaloosa, and he was a great guitar player, too. We got a battle of the bands at the Dew Drop. Big Poppa won. His guitar was much stronger. My guitar player, Lazy Lester, just wasn't in the bracket with that guy Joe. It had to be somebody like Buddy Guy to tackle him. Somebody told me Buddy Guy wasn't working with Big Poppa anymore, and I found him over at his sister's house on Missouri Street. I asked him about playing with me, and we jammed for a good while. Then I went back and booked another battle with Big Poppa. He was surprised to see Buddy walk on stage that night. We battled it out and we won the prize. It was $10 or $12, good money.*

Harp player Raful Neal was Buddy's first partner.

"By the time I first met Buddy, his shy was gone. Yes, his shy was gone. He was PLAYING. And everybody would call him George Guy. 'Oh man, you ought to see George Guy.' Later, they started calling him Buddy. He had a lot of women. And the women he had was getting mad. When he'd get to playing and kicking up his feet, women would go screaming. They was all hot.

"Me and Buddy was coming up fast. Everywhere we'd go, we was getting packed houses. We began to putting a 50-cent charge on the door when he started playing with me. That makes a lot of difference. You could make a little money with them club owners who was getting paid. We'd take the door. It would sometimes be $35-$40, $45, maybe $50. That was enough for us to make $10-$12 then. We done made a double gig. But if you play for what the man give you, he wasn't going to pay any more than $25-$30 for the three of us.

"Buddy would play lead and bass. You'd swear to God we had another guitar."

BUDDY GUY: "When I went on stage, I used to do 'The Things (That) I Used To Do' by Guitar Slim, B.B. King's 'Sweet Little Angel,' 'Buzz On Up The Road' by Bobby Bland and Little Richard's 'Lucille.' Whenever [Little Richard] was playing around, we'd say, 'Damn. We'll go see him 'cause he'd knock you out.'

"We had only a drum and two guitars. I would lead, and Speck, the second guitarist, would play rhythm. He'd get drunk every Friday night. We'd go out 40-50 miles in the country, pull his pants down and stick his butt out the window for about an hour to sober him up."

Buddy Guy first went to Chicago on September 27, 1957. His brother, Sam, took him to the train station.

Buddy took a demo tape of 'Baby Don't You Wanna Come Home' that he had recorded at WXOK, a black-owned radio station in Baton Rouge. Buddy didn't know anyone in Chicago, but he'd made up his mind to go to the town where the biggest names in blues played. Chicago, after all, was where Muddy Waters, Sonny Boy Williamson and Howlin' Wolf recorded. It was the mythical place where the blues artists he'd heard on his father's scratchy radio played every night. It was where young Southern black musicians escaped to find their fortune.

Buddy cut his first demo tape in 1957 at WXOK.

BUDDY GUY: *"In those days, it was much better for a black man to go to Chicago or Milwaukee or some place north. I'd always doubted myself, but I had seen Junior and Muddy come through Louisiana. And people older than me said, 'Man, you can play guitar good enough. If I was you, I'd go north.'"*

Raful Neal stayed behind and raised a family of 10 musicians. He continued to perform well into the 1990s, recording with several of his children. One son, Kenny Neal, records for Alligator Records and tours worldwide.

RAFUL NEAL: *"Me and Buddy had a team going on. Man, he'd come on playing B.B. King's 'Sweet Little Angel.' I'd come on and play that Jimmy Reed shit, that Little Walter shit on the harp. Boy, we'd have the house rocking. We was a good team together. But you know, I'm glad he went to Chicago. He met Junior, and they teamed up. But me and Buddy was a better team than Junior. Yes, we was."*

4 Going To Chicago

"I was shy, and there was so many musicians in Chicago. I had to do like the cat with a dog. A cat knows he can't whip a dog, but he still has to fight. And if you give him a chance, he's faster than a dog. So he has to scratch and bite and get the fuck out of the way."

—Buddy Guy

C hicago was where Buddy felt he had to be. Muddy Waters, Howlin' Wolf, Sonny Boy Williamson and Junior Wells had all moved up from the South. Now they were all playing, recording and living in this big city.

BUDDY GUY: *"They had guitar players there. . .Dave and Louis Myers—two brothers playing with Junior Wells, Little Walter, Magic Sam, Otis Rush. They had a guy named L.C. McKenzie, who could play T-Bone Walker perfectly. I would just walk in the door and see these people and just say, 'Shit, man. I might as well sell my guitar. I don't even have no business in the same town with these people.' But I didn't have a choice. I couldn't find no common labor work."*

Musically, Chicago may have been where Buddy's head and heart were, but still, when he got off the bus, "I felt like a ball in high weeds," he said. Lake Michigan might as well have been an ocean, as mysterious and potentially menacing as his immediate future.

The streets of Chicago fanned out from The Loop in the center of the city at the edge of the lake. To the south and west were the black ghettos and to the north were the white neighborhoods, segregated far more than the plantations of Louisiana. Every day, Buddy would look for work. Every day, he got turned down.

BUDDY GUY: *"A woman walked up to me one night when I first got to Chicago and said, 'You're a good-looking guy. I'd like to take you to a hotel and take you to bed with me.' I didn't have the hotel fare, so the thought of having sex with her didn't cross my mind. I spent most of my money riding the buses and taxis, trying to find a job."*

One ambitious morning, in his best Guitar Slim style, Buddy put on his bright green jacket and red pants and grabbed his guitar, amp and tape he had made at WXOK. He looked up Chess Records in the Yellow Pages and sauntered to their offices at 49th and Cottage Grove, which preceded its more famous location at 2120 Michigan Avenue.

Chess was Chicago's most successful hometown record label. Leonard and Phil Chess, two brothers who immigrated from the Polish/Russian border, had begun the label in 1946 after running several bars that featured live music on the South Side, including the Macamba Nightclub and the 708 Club. Then called Aristocrat, the label originally was designed to record Andrew Tibbs, the house-band vocalist at the Macamba. The label began to grow after Muddy Waters walked in off the street in 1947 and asked to be recorded. Waters became a hit with black record buyers in 1948 with "Feel Like Going Home" and "I Can't Be Satisfied."

But a hit in that market meant thousands of records sold, not hundreds of thousands and certainly not millions. It would be Chuck Berry who bumped the renamed Chess Record Company into that category in 1955 with a song called "Maybellene."

At the 708 Club in 1958, when Buddy performed Mondays, Tuesdays and Thursdays, and Otis Rush played Fridays, Saturdays and Sundays. On piano is Paul Hanken. The man on Buddy's right is identified only as 'Pops,' the cook.

Buddy's smile has always been as flashy as his style.

Muddy Waters had brought Chuck Berry to Leonard Chess along with a song called "Ida Red." The song had already been rejected by Capitol and Mercury Records. Leonard suggested Berry change the name to "Maybellene" and give the country-flavored tune "a bigger beat."

By the time Buddy Guy walked into the Chess offices in 1957, Chess was selling millions of Chuck Berry Rock-and-Roll records. Bo Diddley had the beat the teens wanted. The blues artists who had followed Muddy Waters onto the label and given Chess its initial reputation—Howlin' Wolf, Sonny Boy Williamson and Little Walter—were already eclipsed by the new phenomenon of Rock-and-Roll.

Chess was merely following a national trend that was much stronger than the regional appeal of blues. Elvis Presley had moved beyond his blues roots with hits like "Don't" and "Love Me Tender." Popular black hits were limited to pabulum, novelty and gimmicks, like the Coasters' "Yakety Yak" and the Platters' dreamy "Twilight Time."

The small, unassuming Chess building was two blocks from Chicago's other major independent record company, VeeJay. Buddy presented his tape to Leonard Chess' secretary and took a seat. When she left the reception area, he walked into a studio where he heard some crooning Rock-and-Roll. Being in a recording studio for the first time was fascinating. This was where the magic of the blues was captured. This was where the Wolf howled at the moon. This was where, he imagined, Muddy Waters danced in front of the microphone, moving to the infectious beat, pleading, *Sail on, sail on.*

"Hey man, can I use your guitar and amp?"

Startled, Buddy looked down at the short, stout man. Not about to turn down a request from what may have been a Chess master, he said yes. The guitarist introduced himself as Wayne Bennett, who was cutting a session with the Moonglows.

That was as far as Buddy got with anybody at Chess that day and, he suspected, he wasn't about to hear from the label's president any time in the near future.

Buddy was a new kid in town, and Chess already had an established roster of bluesmen who had migrated to Chicago more than a decade earlier. To Buddy, these artists were gods. They had records that were played on the jukeboxes back home. They were on the same radio stations that played Elvis and Little Richard. What chance did he have against people he'd been listening to as a child on the plantation?

BUDDY GUY: *"If you had written a song that made it up there on the charts, they had all this confidence in you. If I had never written a hit but said I could, it would be like me saying I whupped Mike Tyson. I might be telling the truth.*

"The guy asks you, 'Have you ever done it before?' You say no. He says, 'I can't hire you.' How you gonna learn if somebody don't give you a first chance at it? Every job I'd ever gotten had come through somebody bringing me in. I'd never just walked up and had them say, 'OK, we'll hire you just walking in off the street.'"

In 1958, blues was marketed almost exclusively to blacks on 45-rpm discs recorded by independent companies run on a shoestring budget. The records would often be sold out of the backs of cars to beauty shop owners and Pullman car conductors largely in Chicago, Memphis and New Orleans. They, in turn, would sell them to their customers.

In Chicago, Buddy began refining his flamboyant style, which would captivate a British audience at the famed Klooks Kleek club several years later.

DICK CLARK: *"Those were the glory days of this era of recorded music. The pioneer days. A guy would go in a garage, make a record, go out and sell it."*

By March, after six months in Chicago, Buddy was totally frustrated. Chess Records had not gotten back to him about his tape, and he was unable to find a job. He walked the streets in a daze. His flashy green coat and red pants were dirty and worn, and he shifted his guitar from one hand to the other as he searched his pockets for a dime. If he had one, he was going to call home and admit his failure. Chicago had not been the city of hope he had envisioned. He was ready to tell his mother he was coming home.

"Can you play that thing?" asked a white man, pointing to Buddy's guitar as he walked down the street. His comment jarred Buddy out of his lonely misery.

"What?"

"If you can play that guitar, I'll buy you a drink."

"You buy me a hamburger, and I'll play for you all day," said Buddy, who was not at all sure he could handle alcohol on his empty stomach.

The man refused. "Hell no. A full dog won't hunt. But I will buy you a drink."

A glass of wine was better than nothing in his stomach, Buddy figured. He slipped into a bar with the stranger and gulped down the drink. It hit his empty stomach and went right to his head. But just like the first night at Sitman's, the alcohol drove out his inhibitions, and he rolled off a rendition of "The Things (That) I Used to Do." The stranger was impressed enough to bring Buddy home to introduce him to his wife. The three then headed over to the 708 Club, one of the best-known blues clubs on the South Side. Live blues from the hottest acts—Muddy Waters, Howlin' Wolf, Sonny Boy Williamson, Jimmy Reed—would bellow out of its doors at all hours to accommodate workers getting off the various shifts in the stockyards and steel mills.

In the juke joints of Baton Rouge, the bands simply stood in the corner and played. Here, the bands stood on the counter behind the bar, a platform extending from the back counter across the bar to hold the band leader. Black men and women filled the joint, talking, drinking, laughing, watching and listening to the blues.

Buddy sat down, riveted. The searing guitar ripped through the house. The guitarist recklessly attacked the instrument, seemingly overshadowing technique and style. Buddy had seen that same look in the eyes and body language of Guitar Slim.

"You done me wrong for a long, long time. . . .But baby, love me. Oh please, honey, try. My love for you will never die."

Buddy inched closer to the stage and then realized the guitarist was playing left-handed. The strings were set for a right-handed guitarist, but he was playing upside down and backwards.

"You hear me moanin' and groanin' baby. You know it hurts me deep down inside."

No sooner did the song end than Buddy was being led up to the stage by his new friend. "I got a nigger here who can run you off the stage," he crowed.

Otis Rush, the man playing the guitar, replied, "Bring him on up."

BUDDY GUY: *"Chicago was blowing my mind. I was so excited being around this many guitar players, 'cause you could count the guitar players on one hand where I came from. And to be around that many I knew I was going to learn something I didn't know. In order to learn, I had to join 'em and I was very shy at the time. So I just had to close my eyes and make them come to me, because I couldn't walk up and say, 'Hey, Otis Rush!' Or, 'Hey, Magic Sam!' Or, 'Hey, Earl Hooker.' I was green as a pool table and twice as square."*

Buddy stood on the bar and walked back and forth as he performed "The Things (That) I Used To Do." He followed that up with "Further On Up The Road."

Otis Rush, as much of a Chicago insititution as Buddy Guy, plays his guitar backwards and upside down.

BUDDY GUY: *"The guy who owned the place, Ben Gold, was white, and he'd come in to pick up the receipts. I struck up 'The Things (That) I Used To Do' and he*

came over and said, 'I don't care who that is, hire him.' I got Otis Rush to thank for that. Gold asked me if I had a band. I lied and said I did. I walked back there the next night and admitted I didn't have a band. He got me Fred Below and a piano player, Paul Hanken. He told me all he needed was me. I didn't have to worry about a band."

Two years older than Buddy, Rush was also self-taught and had moved to Chicago in 1948. He'd been playing the 708 Club for two years and could empathize with the importance of a break. In 1956, he'd taken a dub of his blues ballad "I Can't Quit You Baby" to Big Bill Hill at WOPA. Hill played the song to great response, Cobra Records recorded it, and it went on to rise to No. 9 on the R&B charts. It would become Rush's only hit.

BUDDY GUY: *"Within two nights after Otis invited me up to play, this place was full. Everyone was saying, 'Who is this little black so-and-so from Louisiana?' I'm in there trying to get a glimpse of Muddy Waters, and somebody grabbed me from behind and says, 'I'm Muddy Waters. I hear you're hungry.'*

"I said, 'No, I'm not.'

"He slapped me and said, 'Yes, you are. Don't lie to me.'

"Muddy took me into a 1958 Chevy station wagon and made me a salami sandwich. He loved salami. He told me to shut up and don't talk back to him. He told me I wasn't going back to Louisiana.

"How could I say no to Muddy Waters when my dream was just to see him? And for him to ask me to stay in Chicago and not go back to Louisiana was like a mother or father telling you not to go anywhere when you're five years old.

"After I met Muddy, they all started coming 'cause the word was out. 'There's a little black son of a bitch in town who's picking his guitar.' Then up steps Earl Hooker and every other guitar player."

Buddy had undergone his salami blues baptism. Suddenly, he was thrust into a world that only days before had seemed unapproachable. He was playing the 708 Club three nights a week for $25 a night. His heroes were coming to hear him perform, even if they were drinking on his tab. He was also getting work at Pepper's and the Jukebox Lounge at 43rd and Drexel.

One of the musicians who had noticed Buddy was bass player Willie Dixon. Dixon was Leonard Chess' ear to the blues. He was writing a lot of the Chess blues singles and worked with Chess in the studio to get the kind of sound out of their artists that would sell singles.

WILLIE DIXON: *"I had heard Buddy on several occasions. He had a nice audience. Everybody liked him. At that particular time, he couldn't keep time good. His timing wasn't up to par, but he was trying so hard. When you see somebody trying that hard, you know they want to make it."*

Buddy's timing was as unpredictable as John Lee Hooker's. It was as if he were too impatient to get on with the music. If Guitar Slim could grab his audience by turning up the volume and performing in the crowd's face, Buddy would do the same thing, pushing the song, distorting it, shaking it and reforming it to get attention.

Willie Dixon

BUDDY GUY: *"I was trying to ball everything up into one just like the gumbo in Louisiana. Just throw everything in and hope somebody paid attention to it. In my younger days, I was playing like if I didn't get you with my fingers maybe I'd do something different—play a couple of licks with my teeth or sit on it or do something to make somebody notice me. It wasn't like I planned to blow anybody's mind or anything. I was just trying to get attention.*

"I had met so many great guitar players in Chicago. I found I had a lot to learn. I had to do something other than just standing there 'cause people like Earl Hooker, Wayne Bennett and Matt Murphy would stand flat-footed and make me look like a fool trying to play guitar."

Buddy's decreasing shyness and growing sense of bravado was helped along with a slug of alcohol whenever he needed it. Still, he felt he was among scores of guitarists who could play rings around him. There were more blues bars in one block than there were in the entire city of Baton Rouge. The competition was cutthroat. The best guitarist of them all was Earl Hooker.

BUDDY GUY: *"When I came to Chicago I had a slide in my pocket. When I saw Earl Hooker, I just put it back in my pocket. I didn't take it out no more. That guy was incredible. That man had that thing talking like a person singing a lyric. I said to myself, 'I ain't got no business trying to learn how to play slide. I ain't got no business looking at a slide, the way that man plays.'"*

Living Blues magazine called Hooker "the most highly regarded blues guitarist in Chicago." He picked guitar with his teeth, played behind his back and completely abandoned himself to his music. He also played a double-neck guitar, and was one of the first bluesmen to master the wah-wah pedal. If Buddy was in awe of Hooker, the feeling was fairly mutual. After hearing Buddy for the first time one night at the Blue Flame, Hooker waited for Buddy to leave and stole the tubes out of Buddy's amplifier. "I was just trying to get the sound you had," Earl told Buddy sheepishly. "I just borrowed them. That's all."

Still, Buddy felt that to compete with Hooker, he'd have to outdo him, because he believed he couldn't outplay him. By accident, Buddy discovered something that just might do the trick.

Buddy had forgotten to turn his amplifier off and had placed his guitar against it during a break. A woman passed by, her skirt brushing against the strings. The jukebox was playing a Howlin' Wolf song in G. The feedback from the guitar created a constant buzz in G that lasted through the entire number. Buddy went up afterwards and started his set with a sustained ringing G note, fuzzed in feedback.

CHAPTER

5 Timing Is Everything

"Buddy was trying to imitate B.B. King. I used to explain to him I didn't think it was a good idea. B.B. was already popular and when people are doing other people's songs it only pushes the one who is popular."

—Willie Dixon

The big names were playing the 708 Club, Zanzibar's and Smitty's, but many of the best musicians began showing up at the Blue Flame on Sunday afternoons for a battle of the guitars. These cutting contests pitted Chicago's blues guitarists against each other, to see who was faster, wilder, better. But more importantly, they were an excuse to get together in a social setting. The money was nothing, but the winner took home a bottle of whiskey. At least, that was the theory.

Otis Rush introduced Buddy to the Blue Flame. It was packed that Sunday, but through the smoky haze, Buddy could see that many of Chicago's best were in attendance.

There was Howlin' Wolf, all 300-plus pounds of him. With a voice that could cut through a crowd like a 5 o'clock whistle, Wolf had been one of Chess Records' featured artists since his 1951 hit "Moanin' At Midnight." Soon, he'd reach his full potential with songs like "Little Red Rooster" and "Back Door Man," primal works that would someday inspire the Rolling Stones and the Doors.

There was Muddy Waters, the reigning monarch of the Chicago blues, discovered in Mississippi's cotton country nearly two decades earlier by musi-cologist Alan Lomax, who was looking for the next Robert Johnson. Muddy was Chess Records' principal blues performer; Chuck Berry and Bo Diddley may have been making the money for the company, but Muddy was The Man.

Buddy, Muddy Waters and Junior Wells at Antone's in Austin, Texas.

There was Earl Hooker, who had learned to play guitar from Robert Nighthawk. In the early 1940s, Hooker worked the streets of Chicago with Bo Diddley for tips. He toured with Ike Turner in the late 1940s and early 1950s and often worked the clubs with Otis Rush.

Also there that day was harp player Junior Wells. Buddy had seen Junior perform at his high school back in Baton Rouge and knew him from Muddy Waters' band.

And there was "Magic Sam" Maghett, a Blue Flame mainstay, as was Otis Rush.

BUDDY GUY: *"I'll never forget. Magic Sam and Otis Rush were playing the same guitar at the same time. Sam would reach his arms around Otis and play a chord. Then Otis would reach around Sam. They had the place going. It was 2 o'clock on a Sunday afternoon and you couldn't find a seat.*

"Then they hollered, 'What happened to the guy from New Orleans?' I said, 'Hold on!' I took a long cord and a bottle of whiskey into the bathroom, took a drink and came out the door playing. I went out the front door and down the street for about three buildings, playing in the snow. Afterward, they came to me and said, 'How can you be so crazy? What kind of drugs you got?' I told them I was only copying Guitar Slim."

Otis Spann was on piano with Fred Below on bass. Little Walter was blowing harp. When Buddy returned to the club, he launched into "Sweet Little Angel."

This was cutting time. He threw his guitar down on the floor. He stomped on it. He walked over it. Then he hung it up on the rafters out of sight and continued to play.

BUDDY GUY: *"I won the bottle of whiskey, but I never got to drink it. Magic Sam and Otis told me, 'You won it, but it's gone.' They drank it before I had finished my set."*

That shouldn't have been surprising, considering the importance drinking had in blues rites and rituals.

BUDDY GUY: *"I used to tell them, 'I can't be a blues musician,' because those guys would drink from 7 in the morning until the bar closed. Then they'd go to an all-night coffee house 'til 4 in the morning. The bars wouldn't open until 7, so they'd drink two cups of coffee, eat an egg, then go back and open up again.*

"Sonny Boy Williamson used to tell me, 'They don't make men like me anymore. You would rather go to sleep and you can't drink no more. You get drunk, and I'm not even high.'

"There was a hotel above the club in Joliet. I went to bed at 5 o'clock in the morning, left him down there after the band had quit playing for an audience of 12 people. About 8:30 I said, 'Lord, I can't sleep. There's too much damn noise.' I go down and he's still sitting there with these 12-15 people. The man locked him in the club all night. He's still playing and I say, 'Hell, you not gonna be able to play tonight. You know you're gonna be drunk.' He said, 'I'll be sitting right here when you go back to sleep and get up.'

The longer the cord, the further he goes. Outside a New York club, 1989.

"I started at 10 that night, and he was sitting there with a switchblade and his harmonicas on the table. He had one of those small electric fans like the tractor trailers have, nailed above his head, fanning straight down on him and two bottles of whiskey finished. 'Let me know when you're ready to start playing,' he said. I started off. The guy put me to sleep again. He didn't stagger. He didn't miss a note. He didn't slur, blur, nothing. I said to myself, 'Man, you're right. They don't make men like that anymore.'

"He told me a son of a bitch stabbed him in his back somewhere on a boat playing. 'And I went to the motherfucking doctor when I was 24 years old, and the son of a bitch told me, said, "Sonny Boy, if you don't cut that goddamn drinking out, you ain't gonna be around long enough to play your motherfucking harp," and I been playing it ever since. You know where that doctor is who told me that shit?'

"I said, 'No, where?'

"'That son of a bitch been dead. . .and I'm still drinkin'.'"

The Chicago blues scene was far from being financially lucrative. Buddy earned $40 a session at Chess in all-night recording marathons that might generate 10 to 20 takes on four numbers. Promoters sometimes would take Buddy and other blues artists to Texas, Louisiana, Alabama and Mississippi to play 10 or 15 dates and then leave them there with no money.

The hardships created a bond between the people in the band, and simple stories became folklore.

BUDDY GUY: *"Earl Hooker was the type of guy who never did like to pay his sidemen. Every weekend, they'd take this piano player, Cookie, on to Mississippi. They'd go to these country joints and play for the door. They'd make $100 or so, which was good money.*

"Cookie couldn't read or write. So they would run out of money, and everybody would put their last money into gas in Hooker's Cadillac. They'd have about a dollar and change left. Hooker'd say, 'We gonna rush up to the counter and order two or three pops and a loaf of bread.'

"It's July and Cookie got on an overcoat. You know The Man knows some shit is going on in here. They put the overcoat on Cookie and tell him, 'Now Cookie, while we're gettin' bread and pop and got the guy's attention, you go over and steal the finest meat and Vienna sausage in the cans, and put them in your pocket.'

"Cookie says, 'OK,' and goes into the store and winds up in the dog food aisle. That motherfucker got Rival and Alpo, fillin' his pocket with it, and come out the store saying, 'Well look, let's don't stop right now. Let's go about 60 miles and find a big tree where it's cool, and we can sit down and eat.'

"They got about 60 miles down the road, and Cookie spreads the grass back and takes the crackers and starts opening the package. 'Come on Cookie, we got to eat so we won't be late for this gig. Bring the shit out of your pockets.'

"Cookie reaches into the right pocket. Alpo! Outta the other pocket, Rival! Hooker says, 'Man, what you do?' Cookie looks at him, and Hooker starts laughin'. 'You motherfucker, you. Has you never smelled that Rival?'"

CHAPTER 6 — King Of The Blues

"Chess thought all blues was alike, and that anybody singing the blues in any way was copying Muddy Waters. I was trying to explain to them that there was different types of blues and different sounds, but they couldn't understand that."

—Willie Dixon

Buddy wailed every time he played, but one night in particular at the 708 Club, even his energy could not distract the attention focused at the club's entrance. B.B. King, the acknowledged king of the blues, had just walked in.

Like most of the Chicago blues masters, B.B. had grown up a sharecropper in Mississippi, but he had settled in Memphis, not Chicago. His influences were bluesmen Blind Lemon Jefferson, T-Bone Walker and Lonnie Johnson, and jazzmen Charlie Christian and Django Reinhardt. From these influences, he developed a clear, fluid electric style of playing that builds tension, released through a line of halting, stammering declarative phrases. He rose to No. 1 on the R&B charts and stayed there for 18 weeks in 1951 with "Three O'Clock Blues."

B.B. KING: *"Three types of music were dominant in Mississippi when I was growing up. Blues usually was sung by blacks and a few whites. Country was sung by whites and a few blacks, but everybody sang gospel. I was influenced by all three and then later started to be influenced by jazz somewhat because jazz was very heavy down there at the time."*

B.B. King

*With a bleached streak
in his hair, Buddy Guy
celebrates his 22nd
birthday with his
girlfriend, Joyce (seat-
ed in front), B.B. King,
Roosevelt Sykes and
Harold Burrage. The
two other women are
unidentified.*

Even though he averaged nearly 300 one-nighters a year throughout the 1950s, King had never played Chicago. He watched Buddy intently that night. Buddy was gaining a reputation as a hotshot in town, largely due to his emulation of B.B.'s ringing guitar style. For B.B. to show up his first time in Chicago to see the young bluesman was an unquestionable honor. He invited Buddy to open his first Chicago gig at the Trianon Ballroom at 62nd and Collins. The venue held about 1,200 to 1,600 people, and the show was sold out long in advance.

BUDDY GUY: *"B.B. was one of the guys that would bring all of the blacks together, and you'd hardly see a white face. They brought B.B. on first. After he finished, he poured me a glass of whiskey and said, 'Sing my songs.' I went on and sang his songs. I got carried off that stage. He told me that night, 'I want you to be at my hotel tomorrow. We're gonna sit down and I'm gonna show you some things. Then you can take my place. I want you to have that.'*

"The next day we talked for six hours. There was nobody in the hotel room but him and I. It was like a father-and-son talk, and it got rid of a lot of shyness in me. Muddy had gotten me going, and now he was bringing it out. B.B. is the only person who has ever shown me anything on the guitar. Other than what he taught me, I'm completely self-taught. I still play other people's music, but I'm stubborn. I still do it Buddy Guy's way. That day he showed me the straight pick 'cause I didn't play with one.

"He said to me, 'Buddy, if you follow me, you're never going to come out on time. Just play, I'll be there. If you think I'm playing long meter, just back off. Gospel is a longer meter than blues. If you think I'm rushing or leading you, just back off.' When I questioned him about the way he shakes his left hand, he said, 'Buddy, you see I could never learn how to play the slide. So I had to figure how to shake that string as close to the slide as I can.' I said, 'You did the greatest job I've ever seen.'

"Most guitar players set their hands and wrist. I learned to finger-pick first. B.B. told me I'd be much faster with a straight pick. This is true, but I can't seem to set the hand. I play hard and stiff, and break a lot of strings. I can't play like guitarists with a soft touch. I can't seem to find that mellow tone.

"He said he listens to a saxophone solo more than he does a guitar because the horn has what makes him hold a note as long as he does. He said not to listen to guitar players but to horn players. You'll strike me a B.B. King note, then I'll remember Otis Spann or Dr. John on piano, and play it. But piano doesn't stretch like the strings of a guitar. So that becomes a part of me. I'll play that piano lick, but there's also a happiness that comes out of me. I'm happy with you, and then it comes out in my fingers and I can't hold it. I have to let the world know that here I come."

Otis Rush, Magic Sam and Guy were all performing a style of blues that mixed the contemporary B.B. King sting with the Delta-influenced styles of Muddy Waters and Howlin' Wolf. Buddy found the distinctions between styles of blues to be arbitrary inventions of musicologists and critics. Nevertheless, the music of these three acts became known as the West Side sound because all of them performed on the West Side and recorded there for Cobra, a tiny label run out of a storefront on West Roosevelt Road.

If Chess was considered the unquestioned leader among Chicago blues labels, Cobra's reputation was at the opposite extreme. Cobra's Eli Toscano

B.B. King, himself influenced by a wide variety of musical styles, affected several generations of Chicago blues musicians.

*Buddy tunes up
backstage before his
Marquee Club
performance, 1965.*

was a small-time gambler more interested in conning than in producing records. He had never enjoyed success on the charts until Willie Dixon had a falling out with Leonard Chess and subsequently jumped over to Cobra to produce Rush, Sam and Guy, and soul singer Betty Everett.

Eventually, Otis Rush took Buddy into the Cobra studio—a garage behind the store.

BUDDY GUY: *"I went in the back with my guitar, and I started playing B.B. King's 'Sweet 16' by myself. The first note I hit, in walks Eli Toscano with Harold Burrage. Both of them had contracts in their hands, and Harold Burrage was saying, 'Sign him now.'*

"'Who is the motherfucker?' Eli said.

"And Burrage was pointing at the contract saying, 'Sign the motherfucker, man.' Then they brought Willie Dixon in later on, and they started writing songs right there, after I sat there and played for a while.

"I wanted a record out. Eli had Otis and Magic Sam. They looked like the youngest two guys. Freddy King wasn't recording. None of the other younger cats was recording. Those were the two cats that had records out."

Willie Dixon and
Buddy at Legends,
making up a song.

Buddy put out just one single, "I Sit and Cry and Sing the Blues," for the Cobra group, on the company's companion label, Artistic.

WILLIE DIXON: *"That's one of the songs I'd perform in Germany. Everybody liked it so much they had a riot in one theater over it. Every time I'd sing it, somebody would run amuck. Somebody would start shouting or get excited and create some kind of disturbance."*

Buddy was making his mark, even though some musicians were saying his timing was off. Not only had he met his idols, but he had earned the approval of two of the biggest names in the blues world, Muddy Waters and B.B. King. And he had gotten his own record contract and was being produced by the hottest bluesman in the business, Willie Dixon.

CHAPTER 7 Chess Games

> "When I played for Chess, they'd make me play this soft clean stuff, strictly blues guitar, the type of thing they had an idea was going over. In the meantime, I was out there in the clubs saying, 'I want to blast that thing.'"
>
> —Buddy Guy

"I Sit and Cry and Sing the Blues" went nowhere on the charts. Willie Dixon would say years later that it wasn't properly promoted. Then again, Cobra/Artistic's other artists, Otis Rush and Magic Sam, weren't selling records, either. The fact was, if you were a Chicago bluesman, the place to be was Chess Records, home of the blues elite.

Independent labels catered to specialty interests such as Country-Western and Rhythm-and-Blues, a catchall category that included any music performed by blacks. Chess Records had discovered a gold mine in the blues of rural Southern black artists who were migrating to Chicago, Memphis and St. Louis. Muddy Waters had sold 70-80,000 copies of his biggest hits, "Feel Like Going Home" and "I Can't Be Satisfied." Chuck Berry was selling millions; "Maybellene" reached No. 5 on the Billboard charts on August 31, 1955.

By the time Buddy recorded for Cobra, the majors were diligently trying to recapture their dominant position in the record industry by catering to a new audience—teenagers. By stealing the independents' music, watering it down and sanitizing it for suburban teens, the majors were reclaiming their share of the market. Between 1955 and 1959, independents had 101 of the top-10 hits, compared with 46 by the majors. Two years later, the majors had 48 top-10 hits, compared with 45 by the independents.

Chess took the majors' lead and got into doo-wop Rock-and-Roll in a big way. Between 1951 and 1958, it had hits with Bobby Charles ("See You Later Alligator"), Dale Hawkins ("Susie Q"), The Monotones ("Book of Love"), Clarence "Frogman" Henry ("Ain't Got No Home") and the Tune Weavers ("Happy, Happy Birthday Baby").

(Interestingly, Chess Records rejected an offer in 1955 from Sam Phillips of Sun Records in Memphis to buy Elvis Presley's contract, along with those of several other artists who began at Sun. The reason given was that Chess wasn't a "hillbilly" label.)

The majors responded by continuing to have white artists copy and sanitize the music of the hit black artists. Bill Haley and the Comets, who had initially hit with "Rock Around the Clock," successfully covered "See You Later Alligator." Chess counter-covered Gene & Eunice's "Kokomo" with a version by the Flamingos. Both were later checkmated with the same song by Marvin and Johnny on Modern, the Crew Cuts for Mercury, Tony Bennett on Columbia and finally by RCA's Perry Como, who enjoyed the biggest success with the song.

Cobra was faring badly during these top-40 hit wars between the independents and the majors. First, Willie Dixon returned to his old job at Chess. Then, Cobra's head, Eli Toscano was either murdered or died accidentally, depending upon who told the story. Chess was now more than ever Buddy's hope for success.

Dixon now discovered and groomed new talent for Chess, and convinced Leonard that there was room at the label for another blues guitarist. Leonard sent Otis Rush to get Buddy to come over to the Chess label.

Despite this breakthrough, Buddy would still have to struggle with elusive success. Both Dixon and Leonard Chess had strong personalities and opinions and were strongly motivated by the success of Chuck Berry, who was selling more than 10 times the number of records as Muddy Waters.

BUDDY GUY: *"He (Chuck Berry) tried to sell 'Maybellene.' He sold blood for that. He thought up 'School Days.' They asked him what was next. He says, 'Give me five minutes.' So he goes over and sits there while the band begins, 'Up in the morning and out to school.'*

"I was on shows with Chuck Berry, but not as much as Muddy and those guys. Muddy, Little Walter, the Wolf and those was down to earth. If there was a party and a bottle, you had one of them. Chuck was a loner. You'd never catch him in a conversation. I had a drummer, Clifton James, who worked with Chuck. They'd be sitting in the studio, and he'd say, 'Hold it! I'll have you a song in a minute.' He'd go in a corner and sing it just like he did it on the record, quick like a minute. He was a genius at that stuff."

Dixon, a prolific songwriter and bass player, believed in infusing blues with basic truths he called "wisdom in the blues."

WILLIE DIXON: *"Most people never knew the amount of wisdom that's in the blues. Blues is the greatest thing there is because everything that lives likes music, and everybody loves rhythm to a certain extent. Most of the music you hear don't have enough wisdom in 'em. And the wisdom of the blues has always been the main point that people didn't want the world to know about, because the blues has got in it all of black history one way or another. And the blues has always made a statement about the facts of life that the world had never recognized."*

It wasn't enough for Chess and Dixon simply to record their blues artists the way they performed in the bars of Chicago. The label's success with the Rock-and-Roll market had shown that constant dickering with combinations of musicians, arrangements, melodies and lyrics was creating sounds that would sell more records. Actually, the policy wasn't new in 1960. When the label first recorded Muddy Waters in 1948, they placed him with Sunnyland Slim on acoustic piano. Never mind that Muddy and his electric band had justifiably earned the nickname "Head Cutters" for its habit of walking into bars unannounced, setting up, performing, passing the hat and then moving on to three or four bars a night and cleaning up on donations. Chess recorded Muddy with Sunnyland because that's the kind of records the majors were putting out at the time on their "Race" record labels of the 1940s. The Chess blues artists accepted such tinkering because just having a record increased their drawing and selling power. But if the great Muddy Waters was not being recorded the way he sounded with his band in taverns and theaters, what chance did Buddy Guy have?

Buddy strongly believed that to draw an audience, he had to dazzle the crowds with loud music and flashy tricks. Willie Dixon claims to have seen some value in Buddy's flamboyant style.

BUDDY GUY   Chess Recording Artist

WILLIE DIXON: *"Everyone around the West Side of Chicago was telling how Buddy Guy could wield his guitar around, playing upside the wall, even when the music wasn't sounding good. He kept playing until he got it together."*

Leonard Chess still saw it only as useless noise and insisted that Buddy remain more restrained in the studio. As pop music evolved in the 1960s, Chess Records' increasing preoccupation with cashing in on fads like dance crazes, soul music, novelty pop songs and the folk boom put a strain on the relationship it had with its blues roster. Coming on board more than a decade after Chess' other major blues artists, Buddy couldn't expect the same level of paternalistic favor the label was giving Muddy and the Wolf. And not being a rocker or a doo-wop singer, he wasn't cashing in on the teen scene either, although it wasn't for not trying.

BUDDY GUY: *"If I'd have gone to Chess and wrote a hit, they would have stepped me up like Willie Dixon or Chuck Berry and said, 'Let's let Buddy hear this song and see if it's OK.' This was what Willie Dixon did. If you had a good blues song on Cobra or Chess Records, they'd say, 'Let's see what Willie thinks about it,' because he'd been affiliated with a couple of hits. He had wrote some. And when you write some, everybody wants to know what you think."*

Buddy's live performances were gaining him a reputation as a musician to see. Jimmy Rogers, the guitarist who helped formulate the Chicago blues sound with Muddy Waters, said Buddy always put on "a real good show, but the stuff he was doing was stuff people were familiar with in the first place because it came from T-Bone Walker, really. Then, he added B.B. King stuff to it."

Willie Dixon believed in 'the wisdom of the blues.'

Theresa Needham of Theresa's Lounge remembers Buddy exciting the audiences in her club. "He upset the whole house," she told *Living Blues* magazine. "I never heard anybody like him."

BUDDY GUY: *"All these guitar players were saying, 'I gotta see this guy.' They kept coming out, and then they'd say, 'Look, did you hear the way he played that Wolf song? Are they Wolf notes or Buddy notes?' And it just led to their bringing me in. 'He knows how to play. We want him to play.' Muddy used to tell me the importance of having a record on the street was to get the best club jobs and to get the best income from live performances.*

"But I had taken Chicago by storm. I didn't need no damn record. I had every club in Chicago sewed up. Everybody else was sitting in chairs playing. I wasn't getting paid shit. But who was?"

Buddy, now becoming a full-fledged family man—he and his first wife, Joanne, would produce six children—was caught in the Chess dilemma. He was tearing up the live scene, but he didn't fit into Chess' image as a father of the blues or as a Rock-and-Roll stepchild. Instead, he was the sideman they called in for sessions whenever they needed a savvy guitarist who was versatile and could roll with the punches. This led to situations where, in the studio, his guitar sounded cramped and jammed into complex arrangements that often featured three saxophones and a rhythm section.

BUDDY GUY: *"Every time I got a break in the studio or a chance to play with somebody, I was playing almost like an acoustic guitar, because that's how loud they'd let you go. But then, just to play behind the people I admired the most was such a thrill, just to be a part of what they were doing."*

DR. JOHN: *"Can you hear those (early Buddy Guy) records? It sounds like he's compressed to death on some of those records. You feel a guy in there trying to burst out, and he's jammed into a little bitty part of himself that ain't him."*

Chess tried all kinds of things with Buddy. "My Love is Real" was a pleading R&B weeper in the Charles Brown tradition. "Moanin'" was a swing jazz instrumental that had been in the repertoire of Art Blakey's Jazz Messengers. "$100 Bill" was a carbon copy of the soul raveup "Money" and was never released. Then there were the novelty dance tunes like "Hully Gully," "Slop Around" and "American Bandstand," none of which were released as a single.

Mac 'Dr. John' Rebennack

Chess even wanted to give Buddy a new identity.

BUDDY GUY: *"They wanted to change my name to something musical like Muddy Waters or Howlin' Wolf. They wanted my name to be King. There were about 50 of them, anyway. Most aren't still around. But you have Albert King, Eddy King, Freddy King, Earl King, and to me that was enough. But I was going to be Buddy King because everybody wanted to ride on the coattails of B.B. King.*

"I talked to him about it. He said, 'I don't care what you do. I'm already B.B. King. You can be King King if you want.' I said, 'No, I want to stick with Buddy, which my mom knows me by.' My mom gave me that name when I was a baby."

Although music would always come first with him, which contributed to the breakup of his first marriage, Buddy's role at Chess clearly was not to be a headliner. Willie Dixon came to rely upon Buddy for his versatility in sessions with the Chess masters.

WILLIE DIXON: *"Buddy could play just about all the styles. If nobody ever pushes him out there, he'll never play them. Buddy was really a better guitar player than most people estimated. A lot of people can play pretty fair guitar, but they don't have the ideas. Buddy plays anything Muddy could play, only better. After Buddy learned to keep his time together, he was better than all those guys around there. He was better than all of them at Chess. I don't know none that was better than Buddy at Chess."*

Dixon oversaw many of the recordings that often did demonstrate an unmistakable versatility equally as distinctive—but less mannered—as Muddy's or the Wolf's. Early singles like "First Time I Met the Blues" and "When My Left Eye Jumps" projected a heartfelt and often heartsick sentiment that should have made him a candidate to be an R&B hit-maker.

Buddy's first Chess sessions, on March 2, 1960, yielded "First Time I Met the Blues," a song that would prove influential with the British rockers. One of the best early Chess recordings was "Stone Crazy," cut in December 1961. Buddy had written the song and felt it was special. He laid down as many as 20 versions of the cut that night and finished up around 3 a.m. Later, he woke up to the sounds of Chicago disc jockey Bill Hill playing one of the cuts.

BUDDY GUY: *"I said, 'Goddamn, somebody done cut my song.' I didn't even know my own voice. Leonard had released a demo to Bill Hill. He thought he'd hit the radio waves right then, I guess, and overnight, boom, make a success of it.*

"Leonard had said to me, 'We're gonna treat you right,' like they lied to everybody else. Chess was like a test. If the record didn't take off here in Chicago I think they forgot it. They played 'First Time I Met the Blues' a little bit. I don't remember going nowhere with it. I think you hear it more now than you did then."

Muddy Waters always believed in Buddy. So when Ralph Bass and Leonard Chess approached Muddy about doing a new album—*Muddy Waters Folk Singer*—Muddy immediately called Buddy.

BUDDY GUY: *"They wanted Muddy to go to Mississippi and find some guy older than Muddy who could really play acoustic. When Muddy walked in that morning with me, Leonard started calling me names.*

"When they sat down and turned on the tapes, I started playing. They sat there for two hours. Nobody was moving. Leonard finally looks at me, a cigar hanging out of his mouth, and says, 'Do you want a drink, motherfucker?'

"I said nothing.

"'How the fuck you learn this shit? You been here all this goddamn time? We didn't know you could play this shit.'

"I said, 'What do you think? I learned first on an acoustic guitar. That's some of the first stuff I learned.'"

CHAPTER 8 Spreading The Gospel

"In 1957 and 1958 I was writing away to America for Chuck Berry records. Fats Domino and people like that were here, but I never heard of the blues artists. I'd never heard of Howlin' Wolf or Elmore James or any of those people. Bo Diddley sort of appeared briefly. Chuck Berry was the one we all followed. I wrote away to America and waited three months for [Chuck Berry's] *One Dozen Berries*. . . .As far as we knew Buddy Guy was a support guitarist for our gods."

—Bill Wyman

T he first wave of the baby boom generation was now in mid-adolescence, its massive numbers creating an unprecedented social, political and economic force and concomitant source of change. This would greatly affect the world of popular music; although Chess musicians and management continued to struggle in their daily existence, the world that related specifically to the strips of blues clubs on the West and South sides of Chicago was expanding ever larger.

In Chicago, University of Chicago students Mike Bloomfield and Elvin Bishop, along with Paul Butterfield, had discovered the black blues joints, applying what they were absorbing into a crude, honking electric sound.

In London, the Rolling Stones were covering "Shake Your Hips" by Buddy's old friend, Slim Harpo. "Time Is on My Side," a regional hit for Irma Thomas—the queen of New Orleans soul—was becoming a staple of the Stones' live act. Few in their audience realized what they were hearing was reconstituted bar band music from Chicago, Mississippi and New Orleans.

And in Cambridge, Massachusetts, even the vaunted Club 47 was expanding its repertoire of coffeehouse fare from the acoustic blues of Harvard alumnus Tom Rush to include the electric sounds of the Chambers Brothers and John Hammond—son of the John Hammond who had brought Billie Holiday and Bob Dylan to Columbia Records, and who produced Bessie Smith's last recording session there.

As always, commercial forces—largely in the form of Dick Clark's *American Bandstand*—were steering popular music toward the pimple-cream and chewing-gum crowd. Emanating from the ABC network affiliate station in Philadelphia, the weekly show effectively served to commercialize popular music to an unprecedented level. For every genius such as Little Stevie Wonder, there were 10 prefabbed Fabians or Bobby Rydells who reduced American pop to a common denominator.

Elvis Presley had created the mold from which the Philly pretty boys manufactured their image. The persona of the King of Rock-and-Roll was shaped in a Memphis studio when Sam Phillips encouraged the young truck driver to apply his country music talents to Arthur Crudup's "That's All Right, Mama." Presley's rockabilly remake of that Mississippi blues tune helped focus pop music's attention on the electric guitar and riveted attention to Presley's urgent crooning.

DICK CLARK: *"I think ethnic music was exposed in the late 1950s as 'Race' music. It was played on black radio stations. It gave birth to or was part of Rhythm-and-Blues. Rhythm-and-Blues combined itself with country music and became Rock-and-Roll. So, the audience attention went away from the roots. Roots will always be a factional area of music because that's the way it's divided these days with so many choices."*

The college baby-boomers, first weaned on 1950s pop music and then enlightened by the socially relevant folk-blues sounds and lyrics, may not have immediately recognized what was missing. After all, folk music was no more immune to commercial exploitation than blues had been. While acts such as Tom Paxton and Tom Rush were playing the coffeehouses of Harvard Square, the Kingston Trio and Peter, Paul and Mary were selling out college gymnasium concerts.

Bob Dylan, like Presley before him, had success both artistically and commercially in crossing the line from authentic roots. Presley blurred the distinctions between blues and rock; Dylan between folk and rock.

The initial folk boom in the late 1950s relied on slavish copies of earlier traditional folk songs. Dylan showed a mass audience that contemporary lyrics could be as powerful and more relevant than resurrecting the dust-bowl ballads of Woody Guthrie. He was also intrigued with the rock music he was hearing by groups like the Rolling Stones, who were taking the same liberties with blues that he was with folk music. Perhaps because of their folk roots—and their flagrant disregard for tradition—a young group from the West Coast called the Byrds intrigued Dylan. The Byrds' leader was Roger McGuinn, who had been a vocalist in two Kingston Trio soundalike groups, the Limeliters and the Chad Mitchell Trio.

ROGER McGUINN: *"Dylan sent us a copy of 'Mr. Tambourine Man' with Ramblin' Jack Elliott singing harmony. It was five verses long in 2/4 time. It sounded like a folk song. A version that he later released didn't have Ramblin' Jack on it. But it was a nice-sounding folk song. It really didn't sound like a hit, but our manager, Jim Dixon, thought it was going to be a hit. So he made us all audition to see who was gonna sing it, and I got the part. I rearranged it. I changed the time signature to 4/4 and we picked a verse we liked and cut it down for time because radio doesn't like anything longer than two minutes and 30 seconds."*

"Mr. Tambourine Man" was the 14th-best selling pop hit of 1965 and established a precedent for electric guitars in folk music.

ROGER McGUINN: *"I think Dylan saw what I saw which was the Beatles and the Stones. He saw that happening, and it changed the ball game. It went from rock being a manufactured thing, where they'd get a good-looking kid from Philadelphia who couldn't really sing very well, and put him out there as a rock star. Then they'd try and do an Elvis thing with him to where it was really an organic group that had combined elements of folk and bossa nova, jazz and rock, throwing it all together and making a really good blend of stuff. I think Dylan felt the same thing I did. I can't speak for him, but I think he was turned on by the English music scene."*

In July, one month after "Mr. Tambourine Man" made it to No. 1, Dylan appeared at the Newport Folk Festival backed by the Paul Butterfield Blues Band, a racially mixed Chicago group. Dylan got booed. He was also booed that fall when he toured with an electric band that included Levon Helm and Robbie Robertson, who would later form The Band.

But that initial lack of acceptance wouldn't matter in the long run. The folk boom had just been penetrated by the urgency and vitality of electric blues.

It was one thing for American folk music fans to dismiss the importance of Chicago blues, but the British music establishment had been oblivious to the very existence of electric blues. Then, in 1962, Bill Wyman started a rehearsal with his new band by playing Louisiana bluesman Slim Harpo's "I'm a King Bee," and one year later, the Rolling Stones—with Wyman on bass guitar—appeared on the scene.

The Beatles, largely inspired by American roots played by whites (their name was a takeoff on the Crickets, Buddy Holly's band), made it big first, but the Rolling Stones' impact was just as large. In the States, the Stones' first American album, *America's Newest Hitmakers*, contained "I'm a King Bee," Willie Dixon's "I Just Want to Make Love to You," and "Carol" by Chuck Berry.

Bill Wyman

BILL WYMAN: *"They'd never heard the music, so they couldn't relate it to anything. It was just a different music. And the biggest problem was they didn't know how to dance to it because people danced together in those days. They did ballroom* *dancing. They did the Twist for a year and a half, then the Madison where you're in lines and you all do the same thing. But there was no separate dancing as such like there is now. So when we started to play, the rhythms were different. They couldn't dance the bloody fox trot to our music, could they?"*

CHAPTER 9 British Invasion

"All of a sudden, I heard the blues was up north. Someone said, 'Man, you should go up there. They got this Paul Butterfield.' I said, 'Who the hell is this?' I'd seen Mike Bloomfield and them coming in these clubs on the South Side. And in those days every time you saw a white face in one of the black clubs, you thought it was a cop. Those guys didn't come up and say, 'I'm Mike, I'm learning how to play the blues.' They just sat there and listened."

—Buddy Guy

The Rolling Stones, in total awe of the Chicago sound, wanted to capture some of the original Chess magic on record. So it was off to the Windy City in June 1964.

BILL WYMAN: *"In England they had no idea what we were looking for sound-wise, and there was nobody in the studios capable of reproducing that sound. The engineers didn't know what we were after, you know. There was only one guy we worked with who had any idea. And that was Glyn Johns, who worked on some of our early stuff.*

"[When we got to Chess Records in Chicago], we pulled up with the equipment, and we were out there putting the guitars in and the mike stands and amps. Muddy came walking down the street, and he helped us in with it. We were like [in awe]. And he was like, 'Come on, boys. Gimme that. I'll help you.'

"A while earlier, we had been thinking, 'God, suppose we met Muddy Waters and those guys at the studio when we were there?' And there he was helping us with the gear. It was unbelievable. And I remember when I went to do the bass. Ron Malo said, 'No, no! You don't have to do that. See that socket in the wall? Just plug in there.' It was all direct. We'd never recorded direct before. And I just plugged my bass amp into this socket in the wall. And I got a really good bluesy bass sound which was exactly what we were looking for. It was great. We cut 13 to 17 tracks there in two days. And we went back two other times as well."

Buddy didn't know much about the Stones. To him, they were mere novelties.

BUDDY GUY: *"I was over in the booth singing, 'My Time After A While,' and these guys are all lined up against the wall with this long hair. I'm saying, 'What the hell is this?' And all of a sudden, it's the Stones, which I knew a little bit about. You know, the name had been getting around, and I said, 'Oh, Jesus.'*

"Sonny Boy Williamson and Little Walter were in the studio, arguing about some young girl they had down in Kentucky. Walter told Sonny Boy he didn't know the girl, and they got into an argument about it. Sonny Boy did know the girl! When he described her to Walter, he said the first thing the girl ever had was one of his fingers. And he said the second thing the girl ever had was his two fingers. Then he said, 'You know what the third thing was?' And Walter says, 'No! What, motherfucker?' Sonny Boy stuck his tongue out and popped his fingers, walked off and looked around and winked at me.

"The Rolling Stones were all lined up against the wall. They were very young, and they just fell out. They was lying on the floor laughing."

Another young British rock band not yet signed to a recording label was the Yardbirds. Their lead guitarist was a young man who idolized the Chicago blues musicians to the point of slavishly copying their riffs. Eric Clapton had heard Buddy Guy on Chess records he and his friends had imported from America. He could hear enough in Buddy's playing behind Muddy Waters and the Wolf to know he wanted to hear more. The Yardbirds soon would back a British tour by Sonny Boy Williamson—one of Buddy's Chess mates—but the experience proved to be less than pleasurable.

Eric Clapton

ERIC CLAPTON: *"The Yardbirds' manager [was] Lippmann & Rau, [which] put on blues festivals across Europe. They saw the opportunity to kill two birds with one stone and put Sonny Boy Williamson on a tour of Europe and also this group that they were managing to get them more well known and have them back him up. It wasn't a particularly successful marriage.*

"I didn't have a great opinion of Sonny Boy Williamson. I was steeped in blues, but it had to be blues guitar playing. The only harp player I liked was Little Walter. I didn't even like Sonny Boy Williamson I, the original Sonny Boy. So, I wasn't particularly in awe of Sonny Boy Williamson. I found he was a pretty tough character. And that fact made it worse, really. He didn't like us, and we were all a bit scared of him. Plus, the tour went on too long. He subjected us to a few racial humiliations along the line. We'd have to get down on our knees. We were his little white boys. At some point in the act he'd come along one by one and touch us on the shoulder. We'd go down on our knees and play the guitar and he'd walk around and parade around. Being naive and ignorant, we didn't take it too seriously."

Sonny Boy Williamson

It was probably true that Sonny Boy Williamson viewed white blues musicians with contempt, regardless of how talented they were. He once was quoted as saying about one of the many rock groups that backed him, "They want to play the blues so bad, and they play the blues so bad!"

Blues was going upscale in Chicago, expanding to the North Side at a University of Chicago hangout called Big John's. The Byrds and other national touring acts had played there, but most nights were taken up with home-grown blues. Monday was Buddy Guy and Junior Wells. Muddy Waters played Wednesday, the Wolf on Thursday and the Paul Butterfield Blues Band, with guitarist Elvin Bishop, Friday through Sunday.

ELVIN BISHOP: *"It was packed right from the first week every night all night long. It was an idea whose time had come. It was pretty obvious something was happening."*

DR. JOHN: *"Paul Butterfield brought me to Chicago, showing the city off to me. One of the guys that stuck out in my mind was Buddy. His band sounded strong, and they were tight, but they had that looseness of the hip groups. I knew Butter didn't bring me to hear no lemons. He wanted to show off Chicago to me in a way. I used to tell him when I first met him, 'I ain't heard a good act in this town yet.'*

"He wanted me to know this shit was happening still. And he took me to hear

Willie Dixon on standup bass, Muddy Waters and Buddy Guy on acoustic guitars during Muddy Waters Folk Singer *sessions.*

Muddy and all of the cats that I knew that were playing around. Then I'd hear 'em in their settings. He didn't bring me to hear 'em where they worked their jive gigs. He took me where they played their after-hours set or where they were working where I could really hear the cats.

    "I had heard Buddy before in a show or something. It didn't mean the same thing. But that stuck out to me 'cause the cats he was with are strong players and

the shit cut through the meat to the marrow of my bones. It didn't just leave an effect. The cats that hit me that way weren't that many of 'em. It stuck out to me that Buddy and these Chicago cats were really deep into their thing. They were a whole different set of petunias than Albert Collins and those cats. It was like two different universes. The thing that impressed me was all the different kinds of blues Buddy would tangle. I mean, most cats stick to a certain style of thing. Buddy didn't seem to give a damn which kind of way he grabbed somebody. He'd go in all directions. That really impressed me.

"One of the main things I was brainwashed into doing in this business was to listen to everybody and steal what you could from everybody. Early on, one of the first things I heard about Buddy was he was stone down-home, but he was more. Not just the gut-bucket blues, but he had this little sophisticated side to him that even in the most unsophisticated records he was doing, you could hear that potential there so strong you'd wonder why somebody ain't taken it to where he seemed to be leading it."

Buddy had a similar effect on Elvin Bishop.

ELVIN BISHOP: *"He was something in those days. He was so sharp and clean. He really blew my mind. He used to have this girl saxophone player, and they had these arrangements that were a little bit jazzy, but they were real sharp and strong. Just cool, you know. Used to go to the East Side and see him. Man, he was killer. [But his shows] were hit or miss. When you take a lot of risks, you're bound to hit a clinker once in a while, but all and all, it's being a stickler for pure music, and there's appreciating entertainment. You take what you can get with Buddy. It's a whole package, and I happen to think it's beautiful."*

Another white musician, Steve Miller, moved to Chicago in 1964. Miller had met Les Paul when he was five years old, and his father would bring T-Bone Walker to the house. By 15, Miller had performed with Jimmy Reed. In Chicago, he sat in with Howlin' Wolf, Paul Butterfield and, for a short period, worked for Buddy.

STEVE MILLER: *"There were a bunch of bands, and we all just rotated around in a circle to these clubs. I would go and play all these black clubs. It was a novelty because I was a white boy who could play blues and really move the joint. I know it sounds absurd, but if Howlin' Wolf was playing at Big John's, I was trying to get his gig at Club Melody or the Blue Flame or wherever it was.*

"I was playing rhythm guitar in Buddy's band in 1964-65, and we had to have a shot of whiskey after each set. That was the rule in the band.

"Buddy was the guy who told me to call it the Steve Miller Band. I had a talk with him on a bar stool one day and said, 'Well, Buddy, I'm gonna go out to San Francisco and see if I can make it out there.' He was going, 'Steve, let me give you some advice. Call it the Steve Miller Band because you're gonna have lots of different guys come and go in your band. Don't call yourselves the Foghorns or something. Call it the Steve Miller Band and you'll do great.'"

10 The King Of England

"It seemed more like not how much music you made but how much money you were making [that made the difference]."

—Roger McGuinn

Buddy, Earl Hooker, and Otis Rush were among the young Chicago blues artists who, like the British rockers, wanted to use Chicago blues as a stepping stone to the development of a wilder, freer sound. The British, urged on by their young fans, were able to push the limits in concert and on record. But their Chicago counterparts continued to be held back in the studio.

The record companies could call it folk music if they wanted. Academic jazz musicians initially viewed electric blues as a sub-category of jazz. Skiffle bands—combining jazz and New Orleans Rhythm-and-Blues—had been popular in the late 1950s. The electric blues that did get played was often accompanied by jazzy horns and Hammond organs.

Before he joined Cream, Jack Bruce was a standup jazz bass player for the Graham Bond Organization and the Alexis Korner Band, two British groups that mixed jazz and electric blues into what the British called Rhythm-and-Blues, a style more distinctly jazz-oriented than the American version of R&B. Whatever its name, young white audiences—having tuned in to the British invasion—were turning on to it.

JACK BRUCE: *"Although my background was jazz, I was beginning to learn not to be a snob and to find what the real music is. I was learning all the time. So, because there was a lack of experienced [blues] musicians around, they did use jazz players. I remember well when Muddy Waters came to Festival Hall, and he had his own band. That was the first time he came and we were all very disappointed because he didn't play any guitar. I think he thought, 'I don't have to play guitar any more.' And we were all waiting 'cause slide guitar is what we loved. And he didn't touch a guitar."*

The Stones returned to London from their visit to America's Chess studios with secrets behind the gritty blues sound that allowed them to expand on Chicago blues standards. They were also creating original Rock-and-Roll like "(I Can't Get No) Satisfaction" and "Get Off of My Cloud."

The Yardbirds made a similar junket to the Chess studios in 1966.

JEFF BECK: *"I think when we got to Chess Records, I realized I was just copying what already had been done. And then we went from there to Memphis and Sun Records."*

The Yardbirds cut "Shapes of Things" at Chess in 30 minutes and then called on Sam Phillips, the man who had discovered Elvis Presley's blues voice.

JEFF BECK: *"We did 'Train Kept A-Rolling' and I remember to this day Sam Phillips' jargon. He goes, 'You're rushing the beginning. The train ain't here yet. Waaaah. It's coming a long way off now. You're rolling.' He just used to teach me these things. I was going 'Wah-wah.' He goes, 'No, no, no! The train's a long way off. Make it sound like it's coming from 100 miles away.' Right there I was learning a million things."*

Buddy Guy and Jeff Beck

Beck had joined Eric Clapton as second guitarist in the Yardbirds in the spring of 1965. Clapton left the group shortly after seeing Buddy Guy's first British show, following an argument with the rest of the band over the direction of their latest song, "For Your Love." For Clapton, the abrupt change in tempo and style in the middle of the song was too drastic a departure from his beloved blues roots.

JEFF BECK: *"Eric was on 'For Your Love.' One verse was in one tempo and the bridge was in another. At that verse, the record changes rhythm at half a minute. And we realized on the novelty value of that, it must be a good idea to do more records with more quirky things in it like maybe a guitar solo that's totally disparate from the rest of the material."*

Clapton, considering himself a blues purist, strongly disagreed.

ERIC CLAPTON: *"I was very pompous in my attitude toward white blues groups. And I was very racial. I reckoned the Rolling Stones were second rate because they were English. I thought the Butterfield Band was much more genuine. If you were gonna have a white blues band, that was a good white blues band. And to be fair, the Stones always veered on the Rhythm-and-Blues side of things anyway. I excused myself on the grounds I was a purist. I could get away with anything. I was a pure bluesman. That was what my true love was."*

JACK BRUCE: *"We used to have a lot of discussions, in the early days of Cream, about blues. The blues is the basis of everything I do, but I think Eric thought I was disrespectful about blues music, in the sense that a lot of the British bands would cover blues songs note for note, virtually. But for me, I thought the important thing about the blues is the feeling. It's not the fact that it's 12 bars or whatever. It's the feeling that's inherent—that's behind the music or the words. I think that feeling exists in all kinds of music. I think the blues is probably the highest, most developed form of certain scales."*

JEFF BECK: *"Buddy just hit the spot for me. I don't know what it was. It was his youthful vigor, sort of manic stuff and comedy. He had a lot of very exquisite timing and was delightfully out of key sometimes. That's what I found so charming. It was just a hair sharp. It wouldn't have ever been right, had it been dead on the note. From there on, I was like a junkie. I would go around looking for other people to share the same stuff. I was bringing it up to Eric and Jimmy [Page], 'Have you heard this stuff?'"*

In February 1965, Buddy Guy appeared on the British TV show *Ready, Steady, Go,* but very few viewers—if any—could have known. The host, Kathy McGowan, first introduced him as Chuck Berry. Buddy did not correct her, but proceeded to sing his 1960 Chess single, "Let Me Love You Baby." McGowan came back on and apologized for her mistake, saying she meant to say

Wailing on Ready, Steady, Go, *1965.*

Chubby Checker. But Buddy had already left the stage and had never been properly introduced. Clapton, as it turned out, was watching the show.

ERIC CLAPTON: *"So all those people who actually saw the show, even if they liked it or not, will never know who they watched. If it weren't for the fact I already knew who it was, I'd never have known, which is terrible."*

Clapton was surprised at how much more forceful Buddy was on TV than on vinyl.

ERIC CLAPTON: *"I had Buddy's stuff, and my opinion was that he was the most startling new stuff happening, that with Otis Rush. But I didn't think his guitar was recorded very well. I loved what he was doing, but it didn't knock me out much record-wise."*

Buddy headlined at London's Marquee Club on February 25, 1965, about a week after shows by the Who and the Spencer Davis Group. The Chris Barber Band, a jazz-oriented blues group, opened for Buddy. In the audience were, among others, Clapton; Rod Stewart, a young fashion dandy and fanatical fan of Buddy's who was trying to make a dent in the British charts with a cover of "Good Morning, Little School Girl;" Neil Slaven, editor of *R&B Monthly*; and Andrew Lauder, a young out-of-towner anxious to break into the recording business.

Buddy came out on stage wearing a shark-skin suit. His hair was slicked back to show off his high cheekbones and toothy smile. He tore into "Sweet Little 16," "Little Red Rooster," Ray Charles' "What'd I Say," and "Rock Me, Mama." Holding the guitar like a machine gun, he recoiled and shot a blitz of repeating notes which crackled, spit, soared and twisted through the hall. He ran his Stratocaster through his legs, threw it on the floor and swept it up, the feedback careening in mega-decibel agony.

ERIC CLAPTON: *"His look, everything, was right. He had this beautiful baggy shark-skin suit, the strap. We were used to seeing bluesmen come on like Sonny Terry and Brownie McGhee or Josh White. They were all dressed up to be folk-blues musicians, and Buddy came through the way he was. It was such a blast to see him live doing all that pre-Hendrix stuff which he's always done, like playing with his teeth, on the floor and throwing the guitar around."*

Andrew Lauder

ANDREW LAUDER: *"I can remember the first note he played. I looked at the guy next to me, and he turned around and looked at me. Buddy had a real big impression on me. I must say, that whole gig, I thought it was the most amazing thing I'd ever seen. I hadn't heard that sound come out of a guitar before. He was so exciting. You didn't know what he was going to do next."*

In *R&B Monthly*, Slaven wrote, "Much as Blind Lemon Jefferson, Son House and Robert Johnson were mighty influences in their day, B.B. King now sits at the head of an ever-increasing school of young guitarists eager to emulate his vocal and instrumental styles. At the forefront we must inevitably place Buddy Guy, whose recent, all-too-brief visit to these shores gave us an unprecedented example of current Chicago blues. . . .We saw his much-anticipated antics with his guitar. It has to be seen to be believed, and he does well nigh everything but eat it! Eric Clapton, seated next to me, collapsed in frustrated tears."

Ian Anderson, lead vocalist for Jethro Tull, made it a point to see Buddy on one of his early trips to England.

IAN ANDERSON: *"He seemed a lot more cocky and slightly more extroverted, kind of happy frame of mind, which didn't fit with the idea of these occasional blues visitations we had in Europe from rather old men and sometimes old women as well, who had to be led on stage."*

Another young rocker in the audience was Eric Burdon. Burdon and the Animals, a Newcastle rock band, had made the charts with "The House of the Rising Sun," a traditional blues song that originally had been about a New Orleans house of prostitution. The Animals had changed the lyrics so it could be sung from a male point of view.

ERIC BURDON: *"Buddy Guy looked like Jimi Hendrix. He still looks like Hendrix. Sure, his show was a shock. I got shock after shock after shock every week of my life coming across the water. It was great because it was stuff America had rejected and thrown on the trash heap. That was the great thing. All these young white kids in England were into this black thing that no longer mattered to anybody anymore, especially the blacks. These guys were out of work.*

Eric Burdon

"I got [my first American blues records] from a sailor who went to the United States. He lived downstairs from me, and I asked him to bring stuff back that he wasn't particularly interested in. It was [British blues rocker] Alexis Korner who was able to tell me why my records were scratched on one side. He said it was because they used them as packaging for Frank Sinatra and Johnny Ray records."

Slaven was equally excited by the Klooks Kleek show a few nights later. He wrote: "As it happened, lack of space forced Buddy to forego a lot of his antics, and instead he played hell out of his guitar. This was it—the finest ever, the finest we are likely to see or hear for some time.

"The climax of the evening came when a friend from his hometown requested 'Three O'Clock.' After singing two or three verses, Buddy suddenly jumped down amongst the audience. As cascading notes blasted out of his amplifier, he disappeared to the rear of the crowded room, ending up lying flat on his back in a semi-trancelike state, yet still slaughtering his guitar."

Sixteen years later, Slaven's memories remained fresh.

NEIL SLAVEN: *"The reaction was absolutely startling. We'd learned he was a showman with his guitar. Unfortunately, at that time I used the word 'antic,' which may sound a rather dismissive word, but we were aware of the fact he didn't just stand and play. For us to see somebody who just got off the stage and went out into the audience was just totally startling. Totally startling. What we hadn't seen up until then in the correct context was a young Chicago bluesman doing it the way he did it at home."*

Buddy was equally startled by the British blues fans' reactions. He of course knew of the Beatles' success, and when they sent him a telegram wishing him well on his British visit, he began to get the picture. In America, he was a minor figure in a local scene with declining national influence, but here in England, at least, he was revered in the same way he treasured Muddy and the Wolf.

BUDDY GUY: *"When I went into the TV studio [to do* Ready, Steady, Go*], some kids grabbed me and took all the buttons off my suit. At the time, I didn't own but one. I felt very proud. I felt like somebody there. Here were kids 11, 12 and 13 years old, snatching my buttons off. How in the world did they know me? People at home didn't know me. How did they know me there?"*

Dave Peverett, a young singer who would be a founding member of Savoy Brown and Foghat, saw Buddy six or seven times during that first tour of England.

DAVE PEVERETT: *"He's one of my big influences. I saw about every show he did in 1965. A couple of places he played were mod clubs. I was neither a mod nor a rocker. I was a blues fan. Some of the places he played, people didn't know where he was at. Once I went back to meet him, get his autograph and the whole thing. I was talking to him, and he was talking about people like Booker T and the MGs— which then was like new music—rather than talking about Blind Lemon Jefferson. He was talking about soul music, and I was into that as well at the time. I thought it was great. He was a blues man, but he was into other things, too. And that showed. His singing has a lot of that Rhythm-and-Blues thing."*

BUDDY GUY: *"I was always trying to please everybody. Then I came to the conclusion that if I could please everybody, I wouldn't have to play but once in a lifetime. The whole world would listen and then I'd have nothing to do.*

"Finally, I got this in my head: Play what you know is best and forget it. You might make them like it. I wish I'd known that then. I'd have either been worse off or better known internationally. But I was like a turtle that fell back in its shell saying, 'I was wrong.' I can tell by the way they're treating me. I should have stepped back and set in a chair and played."

In the studio, Buddy still seemed to be playing somebody else's music. When he backed Muddy Waters he didn't feel it appropriate to cut loose.

BUDDY GUY: *"I didn't think it was time for me to blast away Muddy Waters because I was so in love with these people. I figured it was just time for me to play with them, not me. But when I wasn't playing for them I figured it was time for me to be Buddy Guy."*

Two months before the Stones visited the Chess studios for the first time, Leonard's son, Marshall, went in and beat his fists on his father's desk. "When are you going to let Buddy cut loose?" he demanded. His father, who still had never been to a club to see Buddy perform live, responded by repeating his belief that Buddy's sound was nothing but noise. That philosophy was never more evident than in a 1964 recording session, after Buddy had spent eight months rehearsing "The Same Thing."

As soon as Buddy put down his first lick in the studio, Leonard Chess stopped it. "No, hold it," he said. "Go get me Muddy Waters." Buddy didn't say a word. Muddy was his hero. Leonard looked at Buddy and said, "You're gonna stay and play, motherfucker." Buddy just shrugged and said, "OK."

WILLIE DIXON: *"Leonard wouldn't let anybody do what they wanted to . . . 'cause he knew nothing about no blues or no music. He had to depend on his staff to tell him everything, because if it was left to him, he would have never got a hit."*

Leonard Chess would eventually realize his mistake in not recognizing Buddy's appeal in the clubs, or that much of the appeal of the British rock bands was based on the kind of "noise" that Buddy was producing live. Still, Chess had not yet released a single album by Buddy Guy. What saved Buddy at Chess was his versatility.

When he returned from England, Buddy recorded five songs for Chess. His guitar was taking on a larger presence, but he continued to be forbidden in the studio from playing it the same way he played it in front of live audiences. As a substitute, he began pouring his emotions into his voice, and his arrangements began to take on a more soulful flavor.

Buddy's frustrations only increased as he saw all these kids from across the ocean flocking to America, ravenously devouring the Chicago blues sound, returning home to record that music, and selling it back to America as the "fab, gear new sound."

BUDDY GUY: *"When those guys was coming out of England, they was putting the juice to the moose. They was getting the stuff I was trying to get the company to let me do. When those guys came into the studio, nobody said, 'Look, I want you to do*

this.' They just said, 'Well, bring me Eric or Beck or Keith,' and they played from the heart what they know.

"The Stones came over to the United States and got Howlin' Wolf's and Muddy's face on television for the first time. White Americans were saying, 'The British are coming out with new music.' The British musicians would come and say, 'No, this is not new. This is Muddy Waters. This is Howlin' Wolf.' The Stones took their name from a Muddy Waters record.

"Somebody else has got to come from another country to tell you what you got? But that's America, man. Nobody knows what they got."

CHAPTER 1

Friendly Chap And The Hoodoo Man

"The one record I got credit for that nobody messed with was 'Stone Crazy.' The rest of 'em I wrote were listed as a 'co-wrote.' Somebody else got their hands on it. There wasn't much I could do. I didn't have the power to say, 'You're lying to me! This is mine!'"

—Buddy Guy

D
elmark Records was a tiny blues and jazz label founded by Bob Koester, who got into the recording business in St. Louis in 1953 when he taped a group called the Windy City Six. By the time Koester had moved to Chicago in 1958, he had recorded Speckled Red, Big Joe Williams, J.D. Short and several other blues and jazz acts. He had seen Junior Wells perform with the Buddy Guy Band at Theresa's and was interested in recording the band just as it performed live.

Unlike Leonard Chess, Koester was not looking for a patented sound that would attract a teen audience. He didn't want to mold the record into a product where the recording process was as important to the finished sound as the music the band played. Nor was he interested in releasing singles for airplay.

BOB KOESTER: *"I didn't quite realize that we were doing something different. I do remember when I presented it to Junior, I said I didn't want him to time his tunes down to 2-1/2 or three minutes."*

Junior wasn't particularly excited about the project at first. He felt it wouldn't go anywhere on the market because Delmark was such a small company known primarily for its esoteric jazz releases. Nevertheless, Junior called Buddy Guy, his old friend and frequent band-mate. Buddy liked the idea of playing with Junior again. The two went way back; Buddy remembered sneaking on the roof of his Baton Rouge high school in 1956 and watching wide-eyed as Junior blew harp in a concert tour that included Sarah Vaughan, the Moonglows, Nappy Brown and Muddy Waters.

JUNIOR WELLS: *"It was called the Rampaging Blues Show. I didn't know Buddy at the time. Buddy said he was there, but didn't have the money to get in. So he was up there peeping through the window on us. I didn't see him."*

By that time, Junior had replaced Little Walter as Muddy Waters' harp player and cut several songs that had established him in the blues community: "Hoodoo Man Blues," "Messin' With the Kid," "Come On in My House" and "Little by Little." Junior had also sat in on the 1960 Chess session that yielded one of Buddy's best singles, "Let Me Love You Baby."

Junior Wells was born two years before Buddy, but had at least 10 more years' experience—and frustrations—by the time they got together. He had grown up across the street from Junior Parker, who gave him his first harmonica lessons before he was 12. (Before Junior was born, his mother had bootlegged whiskey with Sunnyland Slim.)

Junior moved to Chicago in 1941 and was already playing Chicago blues bars by the age of 11. He remembers getting some advice from Muddy Waters.

JUNIOR WELLS: *"He said, 'Hey, you listen to me. I want you to know one thing. You owe your own self nothing. The public makes you or breaks you. And you should never be so busy that you don't have time to talk to the public. You're a public figure.' And I listened to him. He was telling everybody that I was his son, and everybody was saying, 'Is Muddy Waters your daddy?' I said, 'Yeah!'"*

Rose Bowl, Pasadena,
California, 1968

At age 19 in 1953, Junior cut "Hoodoo Man Blues" for United Records, the first successful black-owned record company. It was an instant R&B hit. From there, he bounced from label to label, where company heads kept trying, usually without success, to fit him into some commercially acceptable niche. A 1975 press release from Delmark Records describes Junior's travails: "Over the years, well-intentioned A&R men have tried to shape Junior's abundant talent to their own tastes, and that's why you'll hear Junior with Eric Clapton and the J. Geils Band on Atco, with acoustic guitar and jazz piano on Blue Thumb, with a big brass section on Vanguard, with stock studio rhythm tracks on Mercury, with Memphis Slim on Warner Brothers."

DR. JOHN: *"I can remember Mercury Records looking at Junior Wells as a freak of nature. They used to rib about this cat behind his back like a dog. And when he did 'Messin' with the Kid' and 'Doin' the Do,' they thought they were going to turn him into a James Brown. The joke was no matter how hard he fought 'em, they kept trying. It was an insult to what this cat was about. Every time this cat wanted to go do one thing, they wanted him to do something else. And they never got what they could have out of him. He was never able to communicate to them what he was trying to do, and they didn't give him a chance to."*

Junior was aggressive. He was demanding of his bands. He didn't play favorites. He might use guitarist Lefty Dizz at the Blue Flame, Sammy Layhorn at Pepper's and yet another guitarist somewhere else. If the feeling was right, Junior could make the chemistry work. But he had the true artist's temperament; he could be difficult. Buddy had met Junior at Theresa's Lounge soon after Buddy first came to Chicago, and Junior was initially less than impressed.

JUNIOR WELLS: *"Buddy asked me about playing, and I asked him did he know his timing. He said, 'Ah, my timing is kinda bad,' 'cause his timing was fucked up really bad. But he could play. And I knew he had that ability of doing the thing. I could feel it, 'cause he had what I had inside of me."*

BUDDY GUY: *"In those days, Junior was pretty popular around Chicago, and I imagine he was treating me just like he would anybody else that he didn't know. At that time, you would have people come and say they were a guitar player and they weren't. So I imagine that's what he was trying to tell me. 'I done heard this before! You got to show me!' Then he found out I could play. We laugh about it now. But that's the kind of stuff I would get from him. When I made the rounds with Muddy and everybody else, he came in and heard me. We became good friends."*

JUNIOR WELLS: *"I don't have a brother, but Buddy felt like a brother to me after we got into doing things and got messing around, shucking here and shucking there about this and that. I'll tell Buddy things I won't tell nobody. Buddy talks to me about things he won't talk to nobody else about because he knows it will go no further than what me and him said."*

But it was not always a smooth relationship. The Buddy Guy-Junior Wells years were underscored by artistic tension and personality clashes.

BUDDY GUY: *"When we was in Boston, the guy from the Globe called up and said, 'I understand you guys don't get along.' I don't know how they could get that, you know. As long as I been dealing with this guy, if we didn't get along, you wouldn't see us smiling. So I don't know how people could look at us and feel like we don't get along. I just get tired of Junior sometimes. I look into his face more than I do my wife's."*

Junior had a soft side to him, though. Elvin Bishop recalled a time when he substituted in Junior's band.

ELVIN BISHOP: *"Sammy Layhorn got an offer to make a Southern tour with Muddy. It was paying a couple of bucks more a night, so he went for it, but he was scared to tell Junior. So he told me, 'I got it all straight with Junior. You just go down there and take my place Tuesday night.'*

"I went down and said, 'Sammy sent me to play guitar for you.' He hadn't said shit to Junior. He hadn't said a goddamn thing. Junior took a long look at me, put his arm around my shoulder, took me backstage and started telling me the tunes. I knew most of them because Sammy had schooled me. I was pretty green, and Junior was awfully nice about the whole thing."

Buddy was listed on the first pressings of Delmark's *Hoodoo Man Blues* as "Friendly Chap" because he was under contract to Chess. The other band members were bass player Jack Myers and drummer Billy Warren. Junior dominated in what was essentially a studio jam session, producing music that was more about personalities than formal arrangements.

Junior Wells

JUNIOR WELLS: *"I felt satisfied with it from the first take we did on it. I felt it. When I did 'Hoodoo Man Blues' the first time when I was 19 I felt it, but it didn't do anything for me, you know what I mean?*

"When I go into the studio, I like to have the freedom to do what I'm gonna do. I don't want nobody calling no shots. I'll call my own shots. If you want to call your own shots, then you record. Not me. Bob Koester is that type of person. He says, 'Junior, it's your studio. You do like you wanna. If you feel like you need to do it over again, you do it over again.'"

Junior's timing was incredible. His rhythm was so ingrained that he was often mistaken for James Brown's brother. *"I ain't doing too bad, baby. You know I ain't got no brand new bag,"* he snickers, in a reference to Brown's big hit, on "Snatch It Back and Hold It."

For the title cut, a remake of Junior's 1953 hit, they put Buddy's guitar through an organ amplifier when his guitar amp blew. It gave the cut a shimmering psychedelic effect.

JUNIOR WELLS: *"I heard that sound they was getting out of that, and it gave me a little thing in my whole soul. I felt the hippies would listen to it. Weird sounds like that. It made me feel good because I could feel it. I felt like I could sell it, and the public would really notice it."*

Hoodoo Man Blues became the biggest-selling album for a company that considered 700 sales on Joe Williams "phenomenal." In its first year, *Hoodoo Man Blues* sold fewer copies than *The Legend of Sleepy John Estes*, which sold 1,300. Since then, it has sold more than 1,000 copies each year.

But more importantly, the tiny audiophile label had captured for the first time in the studio the live sound of a working Chicago blues band.

12 Cutting Loose

"I looked out and saw Jimi Hendrix. He beckoned me over. He said, 'I heard the rumor that you been copying me, but pay that no mind. I know where I got mine. Can I play with you?' I said yes."

—Buddy Guy

D ick Waterman, like Bob Koester, was into the blues as a fan first and a businessman second. At a time when the British believed that Big Bill Broonzy was the last of a breed, Waterman was locating blues artists that many in that country assumed were dead. Waterman had rediscovered Son House, and he had booked Arthur "Big Boy" Crudup—the man who inspired Elvis Presley—into coffeehouses, folk festivals and colleges around the country.

Waterman had already managed Junior Wells for a year when he approached Koester about replacing the older acts on his roster with "some young bluesman who wanted to get out there and do it and be willing to go from coast to coast." Koester suggested he check out Buddy Guy. Waterman recalls the night he walked into a half-empty Theresa's Lounge and saw Buddy, playing as if it were the most important gig of his life.

DICK WATERMAN: *"The pipes were about seven or eight feet up, coming down from the ceiling over the musicians' heads. Buddy took his guitar and stuck it up in the pipes, fretted with one hand and whipped the strings with a handkerchief. Sometimes, he'd do it backwards. He would fret right-handed and play left-handed with the guitar stuck upside down in the heating pipes in the low ceiling. That just blew my mind. Buddy was the first guy I ever saw who took the mike stand and ran it across the strings while playing, something a lot of English guitarists later became very innovative doing."*

This was a mere two years after his triumphant tour of England, but Buddy's musical horizons had been looking bleak. He wasn't playing many gigs outside of Chicago any more. Despite his success in England, Buddy was unrecognized beyond a small circle of rock musicians and Chicago club audiences. Young American fans were hypnotized by the direction rock was going with its blues influences, but not at all interested in those blues roots.

BUDDY GUY: *"One night I'd had three glasses of wine. There were six people in the club, but I was playing like there was a house full of people. They had a point in the ceiling above me, and I just took the guitar, put it up there, climbed up and hooked my legs, and this guy looks at me. He didn't say anything to me.*

"The next day I was letting the oil out of one of those city trucks that are too big to be lifted, and I had to use the creeper. This guy came up and just squatted down and looked at me and said, 'Are you Buddy Guy?'

"I said, 'No, George,' 'cause I didn't want anybody to know who I was.

"He said, 'Yeah, you're Buddy Guy. I've come over here to talk to you about going on the road.'

"I said, 'I'm not thinking about the road. I'm trying to take care of myself now. I'm playing here at night and I'm fine.'

"He said, 'No. What time you get off? I wanna talk to you.' I didn't know who he was. I got off that evening, and he was still there. We sat down and talked, and he said, 'How much do you make a year?'

"I was making $2 an hour, but I was playing at night. He told me he'd write a postdated check that would cover more than I would make a year for the year if I would quit the job 'cause it was dangerous. 'If you're working there as a mechanic, you could lose your finger.'

"I said, 'Yeah, but I can lose my life if I'm out there hungry.'"

Buddy told Waterman he'd go with him on his two-week vacation and test the water. If the reaction seemed positive, he'd agree to take on Waterman as his manager.

Buddy packed his bags and headed out to Ann Arbor, Michigan, with a band that included his old friend, saxophone player A.C. Reed.

BUDDY GUY: *"I get to this little place in Ann Arbor called the Canterbury House, and said to the three guys in the band, 'Man, we're gonna blast them out of here. There ain't nothing but white people nowhere. They ain't gonna like the blues. We're gonna get run away from here.'*

"I just went crazy, playing the wild stuff they'd never let me do in the studio, and these kids was going crazy, and I began to cry. So my drummer, Al Duncan, and the bass player, Jack Madison said, 'Hey, you're a fool, man. Play, man! Look at all the pretty women.'

"We had this little bottle of whiskey. They fired me up and gave me a drink and said, 'Keep doin' it.' Al said, 'Man, I never seen anything like this.' The place was run by some minister, with this Catholic-looking suit on. I kept telling my guys, 'Man, I'm religious myself. I can't play on! No blues for these people.'

"'PLAY, MAN!'

"Then I heard three of them arguing. 'He's been watching Hendrix.' Another guy said, 'No, that's who Hendrix been stealing from.'

"I'm saying to my drummer, 'Who's Hendrix?'

"He'd say, 'Hell, I don't know.' So, I asked my bass player, 'Who is he?'

"He said, 'I don't know, man. That's your shit. Just keep playing your shit, man. The hell with Hendrix.'

"So, we kept jamming. I had this little tune I was playing, and I would kick out my leg every once in a while. And I accidentally kicked out my leg. It tripped me, and I hit the bass player. The bass player fell on the drummer, and we three fell as a routine fall. These people cracked up. They thought we did it on purpose.

"I had never seen anything like the reaction we got that night. I had seen one or two white people come in and see me play in the Chicago area like Michael Bloomfield and Paul Butterfield and a few more. But not just a white audience, there just to see me playing."

Al Duncan was so fired up by the performance that he sat up all night drinking and thinking about the wild reaction they'd gotten. The next day would prove to be even more intense, when they drove to a field about 20 miles north of Toronto for the Mariposa Folk Festival. Performers on the bill included Joni Mitchell, Tom Rush, Richie Havens and folk-blues artist Reverend Gary Davis.

When Buddy and his band saw 30,000 folk-music fans in that field, they got nervous and stayed in their car. Every once in a while, they'd get out and pace. Finally, they got called to the stage, the last act of the night.

If ever there was a time for Buddy to cut loose, this was it.

To start the performance, Buddy walked up to the front of the stage, causing the guitar cord to come unplugged from the amp. Buddy pretended to be upset, then went to plug it back in again and again. Soon a stagehand came out with a longer cord, and Buddy went to the far edge of the stage, right up front. Then that came unplugged. Finally, out came the longest cord yet, and the crowd went wild.

At one point, Buddy came forward and leaped right off the front of the stage, which was about six feet off the ground. Then he got under the stage, which was on supports with no front wall. Two spotlights, originating halfway out in the crowd, focused in on him while his band played above. He played with his handkerchief as a guitar pick for a long while, then took off a shoe and banged on the strings. Finally, he got up and moved forward into a snow fence 10 or 12 feet in front of the stage. He tumbled right over it and kept playing. At one point, several fans lifted him atop their shoulders and carried him around, deeper and deeper into the crowd.

Eventually he got to one of the spotlight towers—the one that was focused on the stage—and started climbing. The other spotlight focused on him. He'd climb a few steps at a time, hanging off the ladder to play a few notes. A few more steps, a few more notes. Finally, he was on top, sharing the small space with the spotlight and the spotlight operator, doing a little dance and playing a few riffs, the crowd exploding in astonished cheers.

Then Buddy grabbed his tie and took it off. He took off his jacket, and played some more. He started unbuttoning his shirt, and got his shirt all unbuttoned. Finally, he grabbed for his belt buckle. The spotlight stayed on him for barely a second, then shut right off, completing in an instant the stunning performance, and the crowd was in thunderous, ferocious rapture.

DICK WATERMAN: *"I'll never forget one time, when he opened for the Mothers of Invention at the skating rink in Central Park. He started into a solo and he jumped off the stage, which was not unusual for him to do, but this time, he landed badly and broke a bone in his foot. But he never missed a note. He just kept on playing and started walking through the crowd, and of course I was in charge of reeling his cord in and out. If you looked at him, you could tell he was in so much pain by the way his face was so contorted, but he never stopped his solo."*

Buddy's act was not premeditated or contrived. His style was merely a natural by-product of being self-taught, having a compulsion to play, and being insecure enough to feel that if he didn't dazzle and hypnotize his audience with the flamboyant techniques he'd seen work for Guitar Slim, he'd be buried by competition from guitarists who were better technicians.

Buddy's constant pushing of conventional limits made the Who's destruction of their equipment on stage and Jimi Hendrix's guitar pyre appear contrived by contrast.

Buddy rarely rehearsed his band and, if he did, chances are he wouldn't perform the same songs that night. He never told his band what songs they were about to perform and didn't know himself until he got in front of a crowd. Even then, one number would blend into another. Lyrics were invented on the spot and solos took flight in any direction. This kind of approach has worked for the Grateful Dead for nearly three decades.

Buddy returned to the Chess studios to record with Chess' newest blues musician, a belting songstress named Koko Taylor. She had resisted cutting "Wang Dang Doodle" because she felt it was too weird for her.

KOKO TAYLOR: *"It had all them weird names in there. To me, it was talking about people, pinpointing people like butcher-knife-toting Annie, fast-talking Fanny*

*Buddy played guitar on
Koko Taylor's hit,
"Wang Dang Doodle."*

and all this stuff. I said [to Willie Dixon], 'Where did you come up with all these people? Why do you want me to sing a song like that? I don't want to do a song like that. I'd rather do another.' He said, 'This is a good song. If you do this tune, the people are gonna like it.' Anyway, he encouraged me to do it. I did it. And I tell you, I haven't regretted it yet."

"Wang Dang Doodle" was Chess Records' biggest blues hit of the 1960s. It was also Buddy's final recording with Chess.

BUDDY GUY: *"I used to go down and beg at Leonard's office to see him. I'd go there and ask his secretary, and she'd pick up the phone and say he's not here. He's in the back. I'd just turn around. What the hell could I do?*

"All of a sudden, Willie Dixon called me to meet him at Chess Studios. I looked at all these doors open to this big office with this big presidential looking chair just sitting there, and they made me sit in it.

"They said, 'Listen, you've been telling us about turning the amplifier up and making an album. We're ready.' Leonard had found out that Eric and the Cream was making big records and making millions. Leonard bent over and told me to kick him because he was onto the fact that this type of guitar would sell.

"Leonard told me, 'Before you sign with anybody, we'll match whatever they're giving.' But I'd had big promises made to me before. I said, 'Forget this. You just want to grab hold of me now, and I'll be back on a piece of paper again, and recording in the back room, helping other people record, but no Buddy Guy.' I said, 'Well, I'm not ready now because Vanguard has bought me my first Cadillac.'"

Buddy had just made a deal with Sam Charters of Vanguard for $1,400, and promptly bought himself a brand new, 1967 Cadillac.

13 Identity Crisis

"I played a lot of opening sets at the Fillmore East in New York. I remember one night, B.B. King was out there, and I played with the Who. My name was in small letters, but I had a long, wild night and did a tremendous show. The next night, we went back, and they had my name as big as the Who. B.B. patted me on the back and said, 'That's the way to get 'em, Buddy. That's why I adopted you for my son. Don't stand back there. Burn 'em!'"

—Buddy Guy

The record industry wouldn't recognize Buddy's creative influence on the new musicians until after Jimi Hendrix, Cream and Led Zeppelin had redefined blues-rock music and became superstars. But it wasn't necessarily easy for those new rock stars, who also were forced to battle the industry's resistance against creative spontaneity. However, they proved to be more successful in their struggles than was Buddy.

CARLOS SANTANA: *"Buddy's sound is like a voice. Obviously, he was a first before even Jimi Hendrix. You can tell that Jimi Hendrix emulated a lot of styles and, of course, he took it somewhere else. But Buddy Guy was one of the first ones that turned into an abstract blues. Almost like what Ornette Coleman did to jazz. He started bending the note beyond the tone you're supposed to hear. He's one of the influences in stepping out, in taking the blues somewhere else but still respecting Muddy Waters. Buddy sits on the Mount Olympus of blues. He sits at the same table as Muddy Waters and Little Walter. He plays one note and you forget about the rent."*

*Carlos Santana and
Buddy jam during
1988 San Francisco
Blues Festival.*

Perhaps Buddy could have become a focal point of the new culture instead of Hendrix, who was suddenly taking the masses to places Buddy had discovered a decade earlier—places where Leonard Chess forbade Buddy from going. But had that happened, it's likely Buddy would have become just as frustrated as Hendrix—and as Elvis had before him—by a music industry that demanded he clone himself to duplicate his past successes.

A case can be made that it ultimately killed Hendrix.

Noel Redding, bass player in the Jimi Hendrix Experience, said the recording industry machine pressured Hendrix to reproduce the fiery rock style of playing that was so successful on his first album release, *Are You Experienced?*

NOEL REDDING: *"I saw a contract which talks about that. I think personally Hendrix should have taken a bit of time off and done nothing. What the management and record company wanted was the same quality as* Are You Experienced? *and* Axis: Bold As Love. *But at that point after touring for three years, Hendrix was very tired. The guy should have actually taken some time off to lay back, but I think he was under a bit of pressure."*

Linda Porter, a friend who lived with Jimi in London in 1966, saw Hendrix as confused about his identity as a black guitarist in the white Rock-and-Roll world.

LINDA PORTER: *"Jimi was very into Buddy. He didn't have Buddy's records, but I did. Jimi didn't have any records at all. I remember Buddy's* Stone Crazy *was on a lot. He often played the* Folk Festival of the Blues *album which had a lot of Buddy, and* First Time I Met the Blues.

"I think he was influenced by Buddy in terms of the way Buddy didn't stick to any of the blues guitar rule books. How he would go for it and wail out, and just go beyond any of the structures that were meant to be. That whole flair and showmanship of guitar playing was what really lured Jimi on.

"Jimi loved the blues, but for himself, he felt the blues were too restricting, given their patterns, and the way Buddy disobeyed those patterns was something Jimi could work with, and he went for it and expanded it. Also, Jimi wanted to take it more into the pop music world. Jimi didn't want to be in the blues world. But he certainly used his love for the blues, or his feelings for the blues, and took it into the popular feel.

"Buddy and Otis Rush were Jimi's blues heroes. He didn't have that many black heroes. His heroes in the music world were very white—crazily enough—Bob Dylan, the Beatles.

"I felt Jimi wanted to make it into the white man's world of music. And I felt also there was a double edge to that. There was almost a hostility, in that he wanted to play white man's music better than the white man.

"I think, in a way, Jimi felt he had permission to be flamboyant from seeing and appreciating Buddy. I felt that there was quite a strong link from that point of view. The whole showmanship, that whole distinction from the traditional blues players, was the key to the way Jimi could take the blues and turn them into something else. And I felt Buddy unlocked the door for Jimi to a great extent.

"Buddy's flamboyance, and moving away from the traditional blues manner and method, was something Jimi wanted to do. 'OK, if Buddy's doing it, it must be OK for me to do.' That attitude was there, but I think it was all quite subconscious."

By the time Buddy met Jimi Hendrix, the rock guitarist had scored British hits with "Hey Joe" and "Purple Haze." In the states, Jimi was more myth than reality, a voodoo child who slipped into rock consciousness to change the rules, blur the stereotypes of color and edit the book on rock guitar.

Buddy, on the other hand, was a black man who wanted to be accepted as a bluesman, but he also liked the idea of the white youth culture embracing him. If he was going to compromise himself to get there, it would be through blues-based Rock-and-Roll, not pop. His one bow to his successful rock-star friends was his teasing riff from Cream's "Sunshine of Your Love."

DICK WATERMAN: *"We were probably playing the Fillmore, I don't remember. And Buddy picked up a drum stick, and came to the front of the stage and started to tap the strings with the stick as he made notes with his left hand. He played 'Sunshine of Your Love' slowly. 'Da-da-da-dunh, Dunh-dunh-dunh-da-dah-da.' And the crowd went wild, they went absolutely wild. The blues and psychedelia had been connected before their very eyes by a guy tapping a drumstick on a guitar.*

"Something happened in Buddy like, 'Ooh, what have we here?' I said to him, 'Just hint at it. Don't play it. Just hint that you know it. Just that little opening series of notes. Get in and get out. Just show them, "I can play this white psychedelic shit. I can play white Rock-and-Roll." But then don't get into it because it's gonna be like stepping into a bog, quicksand or whatever. Once you get into it, you can't get out of it. You can't make yourself clean again. Just give them a hint and get back into South Side blues.'"

Buddy didn't exactly listen to his new manager. If it was OK for rock artists to be inspired by blues and weave its influences into their music, why shouldn't he return the favor? Buddy once complimented Clapton on a riff in "Strange Brew." "That lick is so pretty," Buddy told him. Clapton answered, "It should be. It's yours!"

In the early part of his career, though, Clapton thought it sinful to "copy" other musicians' riffs.

Eric Clapton at the Checkerboard, 1986.

ERIC CLAPTON: *"I felt like I was stealing music and got caught at it. It's one of the reasons Cream broke up, because I thought we were getting away with murder, and people were lapping it up. Doing those long extended bullshit solos which would just go off into overindulgence. And people thought it was just marvelous."*

What was stealing to Clapton was considered inspiration by bass player Jack Bruce, who believed Cream had license to go over the edge. He felt the energy that he and drummer Ginger Baker injected into Clapton's blues riffs "gave Eric something that he didn't have before and has not had since—this melange of sanity that he could go out just as far as he was willing to. We'd improvise for 20 minutes."

JACK BRUCE: *"We were kids, and I felt Buddy Guy was a kid. I always felt that energy that he has, the way that he plays. He has a kind of vibrancy. . .which I don't think anybody else has. That has nothing to do with saying he's better. It's just a thing that he has. We all have our own thing. I have a certain kind of emotional thing playing. And I think he very much has that. That's why in those days I felt something we had in common was this emotional vibrancy almost like a nervous way of playing. Sort of wild! I really love that in Buddy's playing. When I play live, I'm not in control. Something else is in control. That's what I like. I'm not saying he's out of control, but something else is taking over. Something else is using the musician in playing the music. I find that very exciting."*

Buddy never experienced the type of conflict that burdened Clapton.

BUDDY GUY: *"The Stones, Eric and many others have done whatever they could for us. Without some of the words and help we got from them, who knows what might have happened? That's why we're such good friends. They just played their music, and the record companies did what they could for them. Some people say, 'How do you feel, 'cause they took your music?' Ain't anybody took nothing. Like B.B. King told me, and Muddy too, everybody learns from somebody."*

Dick Waterman had plugged Buddy into the "underground rock" scene that had sprung up and had become as popular as the British blues-rock in the form of the Grateful Dead, Jefferson Airplane, the Steve Miller Band, the Blues Project, Johnny Winter and Janis Joplin.

Each of these acts was using electric blues as a basis for the new sound. Buddy fit right in at the 1967 Newport Jazz Festival, Bill Graham's Fillmore East (New York City) and West (San Francisco), the Club 47 in Cambridge, Massachusetts, the Scene in New York and several venues in San Francisco and Los Angeles.

Having grown up in the country, Buddy could identify with a youth movement that stripped off the bobby sox to go barefoot, but there were some aspects of the new lifestyle, like drugs, that were not to his liking. He was accustomed to the effects of alcohol, but when the Grateful Dead offered him marijuana, that was something completely different.

BUDDY GUY: *"One of the Grateful Dead came over to me in San Francisco once and said, 'Man, the way you play, we got some stuff. You smoke some of this, and you'll play some stuff you never heard.' I said give it here. I drawed up on this thing twice, the first time in my life, and went back on for my second set, and it did exactly what they told me. I did not know what I played.*

"The next time I saw them, I said, 'If you're gonna offer me that stuff again, I'll kill you.' I don't ever wanna play a set I don't know what I played. It don't do me any good at all not to know what I'm playing. It's no fun like that. It's fun to me when I know I done played a good set, and I have this good feeling at what I've done. Even with cognac, if I get to a point I don't know what I'm doing, then, Buddy, you've had enough of that. I have so much fun playing my music. If I don't enjoy it, then I don't know if you're enjoying it or not. I been like that all my life. I don't want for somebody else to tell me, 'Yeah, you played.' I wanna wake up the next morning and say, 'I know I played last night.' How well? That I'll let somebody else tell me."

That episode only reinforced Buddy's choice of "medicine." Alcohol had been available to him since he was 12. He'd seen his father anesthetize himself with drink just before he died of cancer in 1967. He watched his idols appear to drink themselves into blurred oblivion, only to mount the stage and give stirring performances.

It was part of being a bluesman, inherent to the culture. It's why he had slipped a bottle to an aging Son House shortly before House was to perform at a big festival, compelling Dick Waterman to berate Buddy for it.

BUDDY GUY: *"I said to Waterman, 'What do you expect the man to look forward to if you wait 'til he's 85 years old and bring him out to a concert in front of 50,000 people? He's not looking for a career at 85. He's doing what he'd been doing all his life, playing for the hat.'*

"As a kid when I first learned how to play 'Boogie Chillen,' that's the first thing people used to tell me. 'If you drink, you play that 'Boogie Chillen' all night, and you put your hat down.' I didn't want to be that kind of musician. I said to Waterman, 'Don't stop Son House from having his fun. When he knows he's gotta play, just let him have his two or three drinks and his 15 or 20 minutes, how long it takes him to get high, 'cause you cannot redo him at 85. You can show me the way 'cause I'm 24 or 25. I got 30, 40, if I live that long, maybe 50 years, to try and do some things, but he's not looking for that at 85. He's doing what he's been doing all his life and don't take that away from him.'

"If you live to be 89, you might as well admit it, you live your life. I mean, your days are numbered. Ain't much playing you can do. Ain't much talkin', drinkin'—ain't much nothin', let's face it."

In 1969, Buddy Guy did a concert tour across Canada with Janis Joplin, the Grateful Dead, the Band and Ian and Sylvia. Buddy was in fast company, but his rock-star associations still did not translate into record-label success. The stars were on major labels. Buddy was on a folk label that had gotten into the blues. It was not until after Buddy had left the company that Chess finally released his first album—*Left My Blues in San Francisco*—claiming on first pressings that the material had been cut in 1967. Actually, the material extended back as far as 1962. His first album for Vanguard, *This Is Buddy Guy*, was recorded live at the New Orleans House in Berkeley with a horn section that was performing with him for the first time. Buddy claims that session was marred by too much liquor.

His second Vanguard LP, *A Man and the Blues*, amounted to his best work to date, but it was still less explosive than he might have liked.

BUDDY GUY: *"This was my favorite lineup: Wayne Bennett on guitar, Fred Below on drums and Jack Myers on bass. This was unrehearsed. We just went in and started playing the blues. That's how good these guys were. They could feel what should be played to make the sound right. Otis Spann was on piano. He wasn't just saying, 'I can outplay you.' He was answering me, expressing the feeling I had when I finished the verse. Any other piano player on 'One Room Country Shack' would have run me crazy. He's like just sitting there saying, 'Go ahead on and say what you gotta say. Then, I'll show you how it feels with my fingers.'*

"We all had a bottle of whiskey that day. We was looking at one another. Every once in a while, one of us would smile at the other, like the high sign. 'Go ahead!' Otis Spann was the best pianist I ever heard. When he was ready to play on the low keys, he'd take the whole stool, pick it up and go sit down there. He'd make you feel so good."

Spann's last recording would be with Buddy and Junior in 1970 on Delmark's *South Side Blues Jam.* Bruce Iglauer, who would eventually found Alligator Records, had just arrived in Chicago and was working for Koester during those sessions.

BRUCE IGLAUER: *"Junior had come into the studio not having the slightest idea of what he was going to record. Spann was reminding him of old songs. 'Baby, Please Lend Me Your Love' was done that night. That was Spann's idea, but Junior couldn't remember the words, except that it was a Memphis love song. So he went off on one of those Junior things.*

"He sang, 'I met a big-legged woman, who knocked on my door this morning, and she said, "Junior, you ain't no good."' And during the turnaround, Junior turned around and said to us, 'That's my mother-in-law, and another thing she told me was, "Junior, when you get out of the penitentiary, boy, don't come hanging around my door no more."' And we all said, 'Huh?' That's on the record.

"Junior wanted to do 'Why I Sing the Blues.' That's what ended up as the song, 'Blues for Mayor Daley.' I can't remember if I was there for that song. We did it as direct two-track, so there's no mixing, just editing. That was done in Bob's living room. I was the one who named it 'Blues for Mayor Daley,' because I said, 'If I could bring Mayor Daley to this house, I'd show this old man something about the blues.'"

14 Gathering Moss

"Eric was selling all the records. I was saying, 'Let me learn how to sell a record.' I didn't know how high he was. I was saying, 'You know what you're doing. You're the one that's selling records.'"

—Buddy Guy

Τ he Rolling Stones with whom Buddy and Junior toured Europe in 1970 were not the same kids who had laughed at Sonny Boy Williamson's dirty jokes in the Chess studios in 1964. For one thing, they had lost Brian Jones, the guitarist who had captured the Bo Diddley beat and introduced the sitar to rock music; Jones was one of the first of many rock stars who died from hedonistic excesses. The irony is that deaths such as Jones' only served to increase rock music's lure to the counter-culture, and now the Stones were too famous to hang out with Buddy and Junior.

In many of the places they played, Buddy and Junior weren't advertised at all, and when they were, it was in tiny print. In Italy, the house lights went down in a 12,000-seat amphitheater and cheers filled the air. When five black guys walked out instead of the Stones, the mob began derisively shrieking and whistling.

JUNIOR WELLS: *"The first show we did with the Rolling Stones we went on stage. Boy, we set it on fire with them. After that, not a thing. Every time I started moving across the stage and dancing, they'd take the light off me and put it on Buddy. But I knew it wasn't Mick and wasn't none of them. They're not that type of person."*

Not all in the crowd were rude and dissatisfied. Bill Wyman remembers watching those sets from backstage, hypnotized.

BILL WYMAN: *"Buddy would astound me every night. He'd stand the guitar up and hold it with the cords. Then he'd take his handkerchief out and play the guitar with it—smack the guitar with his handkerchief. That really blew the Germans away. If you're hitting someone or bashing something, they love it."*

BUDDY GUY: *"That tour was one of the most exciting things I ever did. To open for the Rolling Stones was a great experience, but it was one of the hardest things I ever did, because they were so famous. For the 45 minutes we would play, I didn't know what the hell I was doing. These people on that tour were so into the Stones. Whatever we played, people got to know us better, because that's what they did for a lot of people.*
"The handkerchief thing, and whatever else I was doing, was a part of my act to get attention, because I didn't feel I was good enough."

Eric Clapton attended the Paris show strictly to jam with Buddy and Junior, not with the headliners. To him, the Stones had sold out and were no longer true to their blues roots. Ironically, Clapton would soon embrace a non-bluesy sound in his own work.

ERIC CLAPTON: *"I can't remember what we played, but I remember the band was very low amplification and dynamically tight because of that. Everything was*

small when you compared it to what the Stones came on with after. It was like a real minuscule approach and necessary to be that way, I guess. And yet fantastic. I had a great time."

After the set, Clapton put his arm around Buddy and introduced him to the chairman of the board for Atlantic Records, Ahmet Ertegun. "Ahmet," he said, "me and you should record Buddy. He's so fuckin' great!" Ahmet turned and responded, "I'll sign him if you go in the studio and produce it."

"You got a deal," Clapton said. Ahmet then told Dick Waterman to call him when they got back in the States to cut a deal.

Recording for Atlantic Records should have been a giant step up from Vanguard for Buddy. Here was an independent label that had built its initial reputation on black Rhythm-and-Blues and had become a major player in the pop music arena. Finally, Buddy was on the same label as one of his rock-star friends. What he didn't know when he and Junior went into Criteria Recording Studios to cut an album with Clapton for Atlantic after the Stones tour was that Clapton was heavily into his heroin addiction and had neglected to line up a drug connection in the States. As a result, he was unable to function effectively as producer of what could have been Buddy's big break.

ERIC CLAPTON: *"I was about three or four days into withdrawal, and I didn't know the first thing about producing an album. I really had no idea. I'd never done my own albums. I consulted with Tom Dowd. He would ask me which take I liked, and I'd say, 'Well, I think that one.' But I'd never actually sat behind the board. And here I was completely smacked, and no one knew. At least my opinion was that no one knew I was coming off of smack. They didn't know about my habit. So I couldn't speak to anybody about it. I just had to pretend to be ill. And that wasn't hard. I think Tom Dowd may have had a handle on the situation because he said, 'I think you better go home.'*

"I was incredibly in awe of [Buddy], and I was completely underequipped mentally and emotionally in every way to deal with this situation. I shouldn't have been there. I was sweating and dying inside.

"The only thing I remember doing that was instrumental in making the album was that I insisted that Junior use an amp for his harmonica instead of playing into the board, because it seemed that was what they were used to doing. I think they'd made an album for Vanguard where the harp didn't sound very good because it went direct. So the only thing I can be proud of is that I may have reintroduced an old-fashioned recording technique into the game."

The sessions were top-heavy with record executives and producers. Ahmet Ertegun and Jerry Wexler, Atlantic executives, were there. Producer Tom Dowd and members of Clapton's Derek and the Dominos all seemed to be waiting for some direction, and none of them wanted to second-guess what Buddy wanted to do.

Dr. John was on piano for three of the cuts.

DR. JOHN: *"It was craziness. The stuff Buddy would do between the song to be recorded was the stuff. If they'd just let the machines roll, they would have got great records, and not what they got. Record companies do not know about music. They know about selling records. And because they don't know about music, they blow things for guys like Buddy Guy.*

"Buddy's shit comes out fast and when it comes out, you better grab it. He's liable not to do it the same way the next time, and most likely ain't. His shit is original. And even when he does other cats' things, it's his thing anyway, because it's coming from his heart. He'll do things out of other cats' books that's close in and way out but it's still him. And that's the difference between somebody that's an artist and somebody that's just a musician."

Dick Waterman was even more frustrated. He'd heard Chess compress Buddy. He'd listened to Vanguard produce an uptown sound for him that was more show band than it was gritty blues, and as a manager for down-home acoustic artists, he knew Buddy could bridge the gap between traditional and uptown blues. Why didn't anyone else in that studio understand that?

DICK WATERMAN: *"Buddy was noodling and fucking around. It sounded like a dumb rock album. This was not commercial. He was not aggressive. He was not charging forward. The problem was, everybody respected Buddy too much to just say, 'This doesn't have an edge to it. This isn't going to jump out of the radio.' No one wanted to go to Buddy and say, 'This is not cutting it. You gotta get something with some teeth in it, something with more drive, more fire.' Tell him! Buddy was looking for direction. 'Whaddya want?' They're saying, 'This is fine.'"*

ERIC CLAPTON: *"At that time, I was not really developed in style. I think Buddy and I sat down and jammed. I was playing a rhythm part on one of the songs and reading slow blues. At one point I started playing lead around Buddy. My impression was that he was uptight because I was basically mimicking—my style was at that level. I wasn't playing anything of mine. I was mimicking Buddy, and I don't think he liked it."*

Clapton staggered around for three days in a daze before he went home.

Dr. John

DR. JOHN: *"You don't need an Eric Clapton or anybody else playing with Buddy Guy. It's ridiculous. Buddy is enough, and those things are very misrepresentative of what this cat is about."*

Buddy Guy & Junior Wells Play the Blues sat unreleased for two years until the J. Geils Band added instrumental backup to two cuts, "This Old Fool" and "Honeydripper." Still, it was a lethargic disaster mired in drug-induced exhaustion, and it died on the market within two weeks. Buddy had now released products on four separate labels from 1958 to 1972, and none of them had captured the elusive quality that inspired a generation of rockers.

BUDDY GUY: *"I'm sittin' back here and hopin' I get a pretty good record out of this and somebody will recognize me, and I'll have more chances in the studio. Ahmet had promised me another album out of Muscle Shoals. He said, 'I'm the one making hits. All you guys do is play.'*

"How could I go against that? I was trying to get with some decent company so I could get a chance to put out one of my best-playing albums. So I got to sit back and accept what this guy was offering me."

It is ironic that several albums that Buddy had little or no control over came out in the early 1970s, and all were better than the Atlantic LP. Chess

Buddy and Junior vie for the attention of a young blues lover on Buddy's birthday (July 6) at a 1990 Springfield, Massachusetts show.

Records threw a compilation together called *I Was Walking Through the Woods* in 1970. Blue Thumb released an acoustic album with Buddy, Junior Wells and pianist Junior Mance called *Buddy and the Juniors*. Vanguard released *Hold that Plane* in 1972, an album recorded in one day two years earlier. Both Junior and Buddy appear on a 1970 compilation from Vanguard called *The Best of Chicago Blues*, containing the definitive version of B.B. King's "Sweet Little Angel." Buddy also went back into the studios for Bob Koester at Delmark to cut *South Side Blues Jam*.

BILL WYMAN: *"If I was producing, I'd like to spend a little more time working things out and getting it right, 'cause when it's right, it's magnificent. And when it ain't quite right, it's a shame because it could be right. I've got two albums of [Buddy] and Junior that sounded like they weren't quite finished. And they could have been done better because, I mean, the musicianship is there. The talent is there. The songs are there. It could have been a little bit better for a few dollars more. That really disappoints me. We've never had the problem of putting something out and wishing we'd done it properly or better, which I think Buddy might have."*

Buddy had gone from being listed as "Friendly Chap" on Junior's *Hoodoo Man Blues* album to being third in line behind Junior and Otis Spann in big red letters on *South Side Blues Jam*. When Atlantic finally released *Buddy Guy and Junior Wells Sing the Blues*, Buddy had equal billing even if the rather odd cover photo showed the shorter Junior Wells towering over Buddy as he hugged Buddy. They were becoming like brothers; at times tight friends, at others tense rivals. Although each toured Africa on his own one year apart in the late 1960s, they ultimately booked themselves into clubs as a duo following the Stones' European tour and continued to play together for the next decade.

BUDDY GUY: *"You want to know how I really got to know Junior? I had to go almost every weekend to get this motherfucker out of jail. I'd never been locked up in jail before in my life. I'd never seen a cell until I went with him, man. So, two police come one day. The sergeant throws the handcuffs on me saying, 'You're going to jail.'*

"I said, 'What'd I do now?'

"'I'll tell you what later. Come on!' Throws me in the back of the car.

"I said, 'Man, at least I ought to know what I done did to go to jail. Man take me away from a club and ain't saying what I'm arrested for.'

"Said, 'You ain't arrested.'

"'What the hell you got me handcuffed for?'

"'You gonna get your partner out of jail.'

"I said, 'What kind of shit are you talkin' about? What partner? Junior? You all crazy as a motherfucker.'

"They unlocked the handcuffs. Said, 'Yeah, I know you got 250 dollars in your pocket.'

"I said, 'Yeah, I'm gonna keep it.'

"They said, 'No, you gonna get him out.'

"They hold me in the squad car about 45 minutes. They writes me up this pink sheet I ain't never seen like this. I get into the car, and the cop hands it to me and says, 'Now, he belong to you.'

"I said, 'I don't want this motherfucker.'

"'Go back there and get him.'

Junior Wells with the tools of his trade.

"I said OK. Now, this police I know—a friend of ours who comes in and drinks with us—he just sittin' there just smilin' at me.

"'Go on through the gate.'

"I think I had three dollars left in my pocket, you know. So, I go through the motherfucker, and here's a big fat black cat, weighed about 300 pounds back there, with a big key on his finger, just twirlin' it, and looks at me and says, 'Let me see that paper.'

"I showed him the paper. I said, 'I come to get him out.'

"And he stood there looking at me in my eye about 10 minutes. Didn't say a damn thing, man. Say, 'You sure you come here to get him out?'

"I said yeah.

"'You ain't showing me you sure you come to get him out!'

"I said, 'What the hell, I showed you the color paper you want to see.'

"Said, 'You gotta show me somethin' green for me to turn this key.'

"I said, 'Man, I don't have a motherfuckin' quarter as it is. Got my last nickel to get him out.'

"Junior's lying up there on the bed like this, man, drunk as a motherfucker.

"'Well, you better wake him up, because he probably got five or 10 in his pocket. Otherwise, I ain't gonna open the gate.'

"So, he say, 'Well, wake him up,' and I didn't even know the cells lock by themselves, you know. He slid the son of a bitch back, and that door started comin' closed.

"I said, 'Hell, no. You wake him up. You ain't gonna lock that motherfucker on me!'

"And I go wake this motherfucker up.

"'What? What? What you want?'

"I said to Junior, 'Look in your pocket and see if you got 10 dollars.'

"You know what Junior told me?

"'I don't give you a goddamn thing!'

"I'm not lyin. Son of a bitch. Raisin' him all my life, man!"

15 Stone Crazy

"I may not get rich playing small clubs, but there's something about small places I like. At least I can get close to the people."

—Buddy Guy

I n October 1972, Buddy bought a South Side blues bar called the Checkerboard at 423 East 43rd Street, the heart of a decaying neighborhood. But there was certainly nothing dead about this bar. It became the place to be for many visiting rock stars whose primary mode of transportation would be a limousine; Jimmy Page and Robert Plant of Led Zeppelin and Ron Wood of the Rolling Stones frequently stopped by. James Cotton, Lefty Dizz, Carey Bell and Junior Wells were all regulars, and Hound Dog Taylor had a regular Monday morning blues jam.

BUDDY GUY: *"The first year I opened the Checkerboard, burglars broke in so much I put up security gates. They'd screw them off and go in there. Every time it would cost me $80-100 to put it back on.*

"I said, 'Shit, I'm losing more money buying gates than they get when they go in the tavern.' So I took a big pad and wrote a note: 'Do not break the front gate open. Go around to the back. The door's already open. Walk in and get what you want.'

"Then, the motherfuckers quit breaking in. I'm not lyin'."

As club owner, Buddy Guy tended to duties far removed from just playing the blues.

Bruce Iglauer would often come in to catch Hound Dog Taylor. When he couldn't convince Bob Koester to record the raw slide guitarist, he took a $1,300 inheritance and produced the record himself, releasing it as the first record on his Alligator label.

BRUCE IGLAUER: *"I remember the time Buddy was playing at the Checkerboard, before they knocked down the wall of the other building. It was a real small bandstand, and Buddy said, 'Let's get down so low that you can hear a rat piss on the floor.' Then I went in the men's room, and there was a giant rat. You can imagine my surprise! I was prepared to leave if the rat needed the men's room more than I did."*

Buddy was motivated to buy the club partly because his first wife, Joanne, didn't want him on the road. But he wasn't making enough from the club to stay home. Even if he went back to being a mechanic and came home every night, he couldn't make enough money to support his family. Tension with Joanne grew, and Buddy's doctor told him the stress was giving him high blood pressure, the same condition that probably contributed to his mother's stroke. Despite being the father to six children, Buddy felt he had no choice but to end his marriage.

BUDDY GUY: *"I left because there was no way to get along. There was always fighting. That's when I discovered I had hypertension. I discussed it with six or* *seven doctors, and they told me, 'One way or another, you're gonna have to stop playing or leave her alone.' I'm so involved with music, and she'd gotten to the point where I wasn't satisfying her when I stayed home, and I wasn't satisfying her when I was out on the road. So I was too far gone to start another career in something else."*

In 1974, one year before his divorce from Joanne, Buddy and Junior played at the Montreux Jazz Festival in Switzerland with their old friends Muddy Waters, Pinetop Perkins on piano and Bill Wyman on bass. Portions of that performance were later released on an album called *Drinkin' TNT 'n' Smokin' Dynamite.*

BILL WYMAN: *"I was phoned up by [promoter] Claude Nobbs in the summer of 1974, and Claude said to me, 'Do you want to play at the Montreux Jazz Festival?' I said, 'Love to. Who with?' And he said, 'Could you put a rhythm section together for me to support Muddy Waters?' And I went, 'Yup.'*

"He said, 'Buddy Guy and Junior Wells are going to be supporting as well, with Pinetop Perkins on piano.' I had a friend over staying with me in the South of France. That's where I was living. It was Dallas Taylor of Crosby, Stills, Nash and Young—the drummer. Plays great shuffle.

"So I thought, he'll do. I asked him if he wanted to do it. He said yeah. And I flew over a friend of mine, Terry Taylor, no relation. He works with me on projects and has for many years. A great guitar player. Plays blues, country, classical, folk, slide, the lot.

"So, the three of us went to Montreux, and we set up a rehearsal with Muddy. We got up there and met Buddy again, and Junior and Pinetop. We rehearsed two halves of two numbers. It was like 20 bars of two songs. And Muddy said, 'Great! That will do.' Terry Taylor was playing very nice slide.

"We went back to the hotel with Buddy and Junior. They said, 'Look, we don't like our backing group. Would you like to back us, too, on the first set?'

"'Delighted!' So we just went on, and we didn't really have a rehearsal with them either. We went on the next day and did the whole set. The first half, of about an hour and a half, was Buddy and Junior with Pinetop and us three. Then the bunch of us backed Muddy for the second half, of about another hour or hour and a half. Buddy was just counting the times in, and Dallas Taylor, the drummer, was really good, because he had to get it the first time, whatever it was. And it worked really good. In the last number, Muddy got out of his chair and went across the stage and started dancing."

BUDDY GUY: *"Nothing was planned. We got there and found out they was looking for somebody to play blues. I said, 'You're gonna hear some blues now.' All that stuff wasn't rehearsed or nothing. They just called those guys in [Terry Taylor on rhythm guitar, Dallas Taylor on drums]. That's to show you how tight they were on black blues. Those guys know that shit, man, as well as any of us. Yes, they do. I'm not ashamed to say so. I'm here to give credit where credit is due. We'd just call the keys.*

"'What you playing?'

"'I'm playing a Junior Wells number.'

"'Play it! I got it.'

"It was as simple as that."

By the mid-1970s, the world of popular music was changing ever still. The blues influence again was being reduced to a formula that had nothing in common with the sounds spilling into the streets of South Side Chicago. Disco ruled with its anonymous releases featuring studio-produced sounds, where the producer had become more important than the artist. Buddy had lost all hope of producing a studio record that captured his sound.

BUDDY GUY: *"Disco knocked everything out for awhile. It looked like blues had died. For once in my life I got disgusted. It just looked like my mind was gonna go blank and say, 'Buddy, no matter how hard you play, you're not good enough.' Then I woke up one morning and said, 'You remember how you walked out of the bar and went out in the snow and these people were supporting you then. If you keep playing, somebody will like you.'"*

Kenny Neal, the son of Buddy's old Baton Rouge band-mate Raful Neal, joined Buddy's band in 1976. Neal quickly noticed Buddy's rut.

KENNY NEAL: *"Buddy was already established as the leader in 1976. He didn't have to push as hard. He was on cruise. He was just making his next gig. He wasn't trying to kick down any doors."*

BUDDY GUY: *"Probably 1977-79 could be the worst years. I played a lot at the club. I would go out and play California two or three days with no band. They'd call me and Junior out and hook up some guys to play. I didn't like that 'cause a lot of the guys they put us together with didn't feel us like we wanted. It made us sound bad. Then the word got out that we were through 'cause we didn't sound like we used to. So I just kept myself strong and didn't let nobody tell me I wasn't playing. I waited like you always do when you're a blues player."*

Buddy Guy and Junior Wells developed tight chemistry during their years together, but with it came great tension.

Because *Hoodoo Man Blues* was such a recording landmark and the Rolling Stones tour was such a visible pairing of Buddy and Junior, the public perpetually thinks of them as a duo. But that act, which would later be known by some as "The Original Blues Brothers," was never really intended to be permanent. That it lasted nearly 10 years, through the end of the 1970s, was probably more a matter of convenience than anything else.

DICK WATERMAN: *"Buddy and Junior went on much too long. Basically, it stopped working, and they quit."*

JSP from England recorded Buddy live at the Checkerboard, promising an American release. But *Live at the Checkerboard* came out only in England in 1978. *The Original Blues Brothers* was simply a Chicago Blues Festival performance captured on an amateur tape recorder in 1963. London labels were bootlegging Buddy's early material without his permission.

BUDDY GUY: *"Several times I thought of just going and making a record label myself. It might do as well as Sunnyland Slim and others had done. I could take 'em around and sell 'em off the stage. I'd do better than I'm doing with these people 'cause I don't get shit from them. At least I'd get $3, $4 or $5 back off my record myself."*

While on tour in France in 1979, Buddy was asked by promoter Didier Tricard if he wanted to record an album. Half jokingly, Buddy agreed, but only if Tricard would name the label after his mother, Isabell. In the middle of the tour, Buddy, with his brother Phil on guitar, bass player J.W. Williams and drummer Ray Allison, walked into a Toulouse studio to lay down some tracks.

Buddy always plays to the crowd, and sometimes, in the crowd.

BUDDY GUY: *"I had the freedom to be myself for the first time on* Stone Crazy. *We just went in there. . . .We didn't plan any of the songs. We didn't go back over nothin'. We didn't have a guy saying this could've been a little tighter. We just went into the studio and said, 'Let's play.' And that's what I did. I had total freedom. There was nobody out there but me and my band. We made this album in one day."*

Stone Crazy was drastically different from Buddy's previous recordings. The album contained the first recorded hint of his true appeal.

The album ends with Buddy singing, *"Lord, I was blind/I could not see/But as long as I play the blues/It's all right with me."*

In the eye of the disco hurricane, Buddy had recorded his most basic, honest record to date. For the first time, the awesome power of his multi-faceted guitar was captured on vinyl at a time when synthetic melodies, electronic rhythms and computerized vocals had taken popular music to its lowest lows since Buddy first recorded for Chess in 1960.

In many ways, *Stone Crazy* was like many of his previous recordings: captured on the fly, recorded in one session, with little pre-planning or fore-thought. There was one critical difference: This was Buddy's show.

Stone Crazy communicated to the world what Clapton, Beck, Bruce, Richards, Wood, Wyman, Dr. John, Steve Miller, Paul Butterfield, Elvin Bishop and countless others already knew. Buddy had invented a new vocabulary for the guitar and turned it into a solo orchestra.

In 1981, Alligator Records rereleased *Stone Crazy* in the United States, further confirming Bruce Iglauer's label as the rightful successor to Chess Records.

Like Leonard Chess, Iglauer was a white businessman who loved the blues. His strategy from the start had been to record down-home electric blues for a white rock audience under the banner of "house-rocking music," named after the House Rockers, Hound Dog Taylor's backup band.

BRUCE IGLAUER: *"Buddy is able to summon up, apparently at will, an intensity of emotion that would be the envy of any great artist. If blues is, above all, emotion, and an expression of emotion, Buddy is by that standard a great artist, because his music, when it connects, is overwhelmingly emotional—both his playing and singing. And they work together perfectly. His voice and guitar are perfect complements to one another. He can always give you the impression, especially in his singing, that he believes what he's singing, even if the words aren't coherent.*

Bruce Iglauer

"He doesn't always give you the impression that he believes what he's playing, but when it works, he does it overwhelmingly. Like his stuttering, the musical stuttering. The length of time he can pause, the way he'll lay a silence against a flurry of notes, the way a note that apparently is randomly chosen from a run suddenly becomes important as though the thought or feeling had just leaped into his hands, and he can't control it. So, he'll worry about or squeeze or shake a note that wouldn't appear to be the note a normal blues player would choose to land on and work with. There's a sense of discovery with Buddy—not always, but sometimes— that his hands are doing things his mind isn't controlling. The intellect is over-whelmed by emotions. Those are great moments of Buddy Guy and great moments of blues in general."

However, Buddy's manager, Waterman, was having conflicting personal and professional feelings.

DICK WATERMAN: *"He was technically brilliant with an intellectual creativity. To see him on stage jamming with Hendrix or Clapton [was like watching] a bull fight. It was just transcendent. But at a certain point he needed to get down and get gritty. Maybe it was my fault. I couldn't give him the career guidance to take him to the second stage."*

Waterman felt that Buddy was straying too far from what he did best; that is, to wail on the guitar as only he could, improvising every time he took off on a solo. Waterman had also heard complaints that he and Junior were going through the motions, doing the minimum. And there was the popular, nagging question of whether Buddy was trying to copy B.B. King.

DICK WATERMAN: *"As long as the innovator is still doing it, you're always going to be a copy. You may be the best copy ever, but you're always going to be a copy. You need material to showcase your God-given ability to be a different guitarist. In other words, when Buddy Guy would start flying that filigree of notes, flying up the neck of the guitar, something made Clapton, [Jimmy] Page, [Albert] Lee and all those people just stop and say, 'Wow! Nobody does it like he does it.'*

"But when you say, 'I'm going to sing "Sweet Little Angel" just like B.B.,' you're not playing to your strong suit. You're throwing away your advantage and burdening yourself by going into someone else's territory. What Buddy Guy did best was to take obscure blues songs, sing them well and make them memorable with creative guitar solos that were ever-changing."

Since the late 1960s, Waterman had been dating Bonnie Raitt, then a Radcliffe student 15 years his junior. She had accompanied Waterman to various blues festivals as well as on the European Stones tour and had seen the blues from an insider's perspective. Now she was concentrating on her own career. She was recording for Warner Brothers, and Buddy felt that Waterman was concentrating too much on her, or at least not enough on Junior Wells and Buddy Guy.

Hanging out with Bonnie Raitt.

So when Buddy struck up a conversation one night with a lawyer in a Chicago bar, it marked the beginning of a friendship that would grow into a convenient, yet professional relationship.

Marty Salzman had grown up listening to Eric Clapton and the Stones. He'd seen his first blues show at Chicago's Regal Theater at age 16 and could appreciate both rock and blues. He also was bored with the mundane clients he had in his practice.

BUDDY GUY: *"The Stones sent me to come out to their concert in 1981. Marty wanted to meet them. So, he said, 'I wanna go with you.' When he got to the door, they opened it to let me in, and wanted to know who the hell he was. They weren't gonna let him in. I said, 'That's my manager.'"*

Marty was totally shocked. "Up to that moment I was never his manager," he said. "I had been his lawyer for the past year. Management just hadn't been discussed."

As Buddy's new manager, Marty was determined to leverage Buddy's musical reputation and the rock stars' fascination with him into a ticket to ride in fast circles. Why shouldn't Buddy be able to increase his visibility to the general public through his association with his famous friends?

16 On The Brink

"Buddy fits all over the place. He doesn't just fit in one place. A lot of people who claim to be purists forget that those guys they're so pure about were coming up making up stuff as they went along. What does a purist do? That's my question."

—Stevie Ray Vaughan

I n the 1980s, two major artists, Stevie Ray Vaughan and Robert Cray, joined Eric Clapton in bringing blues back to pop music. Once again, the music industry would feel the effects of fans rebounding against pop formulas and returning to the blues. Once again, the major rock artists leading this movement were Buddy Guy fans. This time, Marty Salzman was managing Buddy and committed to using Buddy's rock-star connections by turning Clapton, Vaughan and Cray fans into Buddy Guy fans.

Stevie Ray Vaughan reinforced the connection between blues and rock in a flaming style that more closely copied Buddy than any of the rockers who preceded him. Stevie was the first major rock act to cover Buddy Guy songs. He had great style and talent, but he understood his limitations in trying to stretch his feelings across a spectrum as wide as Buddy did, making up in volume and intensity of attack what he lacked in delicacy.

STEVIE RAY VAUGHAN: *"It's kind of hard to forget the first time I heard Buddy Guy. It was Buddy Guy's* A Man and the Blues. *My brother, Jimmie, had brought it home. I liked that one. I liked* I Was Walking Through the Woods. *I liked the San Francisco album. I like everything I've ever heard by Buddy Guy, to tell you the truth. And I always have. He just sounded real as opposed to a lot of the other shit I heard on the radio. I never liked a lot of the stuff I heard on the radio."*

Robert Cray, like Clapton, was more structured and studied in his approach. His blues compositions tended to tell complex stories while mixing blues guitar with heavy soul influences.

ROBERT CRAY: *"Buddy lived that life. It's far, far different than mine. It has a whole lot to do with the way he plays, where his roots come from. Also, having played with the masters."*

In 1983, HighTone Records, a tiny roots-music label in Oakland, California, released its first record, Robert Cray's *Bad Influence*. This introduced a bluesman who had been as influenced by the Stax soul sound as he was by the growing number of blues artists with whom he jammed. His praises were being sung by such artists as Jimmie Vaughan and John Lee Hooker. He was also winning over radio programmers with a polished sound.

ROBERT CRAY: *"Growing up, my father had gospel records. He had blues. He had people like Miles Davis, and he had some of the early Rhythm-and-Blues stuff from New Orleans, and some of the current soul things from the 1960s. So, all that music was around when I was growing up. When I started playing guitar in 1965, I played everything that was on the radio, from Wilson Pickett to who knows. It wasn't until right before I joined a band in my high school days that I started listening to blues on my own. I had some friends who were playing guitar also. And they were sitting around listening to B.B. King and Buddy Guy and Magic Sam. So I joined right along with them.*

"My list of favorite guitar players includes Albert King, who bends strings like nobody's business; B.B. King, who is sweet talkin'; Otis Rush is Mr. Cool. And then you got Buddy Guy at the opposite end. He can do all that stuff and just cram it down your throat. I like to call him maniacal in a way, because his guitar playing just seems—when his solos start off, they just seem to laugh from outer space. They just come in and take you away. He plays at certain points so frantically and so quick, and his solos mean so much that it's just unbelievable."

The Fabulous Thunderbirds had released four albums by 1983, when lead guitarist Jimmie Vaughan's younger brother, Stevie Ray, was picked up by David Bowie to play lead guitar on his *Let's Dance* album. Bowie had seen

Hubert Sumlin, Buddy, Jimmy Rogers and Pinetop Perkins at Antone's.

*Even David Bowie
can sing the blues.*

Vaughan at the Montreux Jazz Festival the year before, and been so impressed with the unsigned artist from Austin that he asked him to come to work. But when it came time to tour, Bowie got snubbed. Stevie Ray had other fires to set. He wanted to put all his time into his first album, *Texas Flood,* released by Epic Records, a major label. It featured Double Trouble, a band Stevie named after an old Otis Rush tune, and contained one Buddy Guy song, "Mary Had A Little Lamb."

STEVIE RAY VAUGHAN: *"What Jimmie was bringing home was incredible. Here he was, a younger teenager, playing his ass off, and listening to everybody from Buddy to B.B. King, the Wolf, Muddy Waters, Django Reinhardt, Kenny Burrell, Wes Montgomery and the Beatles and Hendrix. It was, like, everybody. So even though I really like what purists do, I never found a real good reason to have to do with that, because I heard a lot of different things at the same time and saw where at least some of it came from."*

As did Buddy, Stevie refused to stay within the lines when he colored his blues. His wild regalia and manic guitar runs soon made him the new darling of the guitar-loving rock set. A 1983 Epic Records press release credited him with being "single-handedly responsible for resurrecting the blues in 1983." *Texas Flood* became the first blues LP ever to win "Best Guitar Album" in *Guitar Player* magazine's annual readers' poll. Mick Jagger appeared in the Beacon Theater to see Stevie Ray in New York and had to show his American Express Card for identification before the security guards would let him backstage.

In 1984, Alligator released its first Johnny Winter album, *Guitar Slinger.* It broke convention for the label, because Winter was better known as a rock guitarist than for his Texas-based blues roots. It became Alligator's first top-200 record on the *Billboard* magazine charts, fueling Bruce Iglauer's ambitions: He wanted to record Buddy Guy. Buddy was nervous about maintaining the artistic control he'd had on *Stone Crazy,* and Marty assured him that a major label deal couldn't be far off.

MARTY SALZMAN: *"I was very naive. I thought it was going to be simple. Buddy Guy! I thought they were going to fall all over each other to try and get to Buddy, especially on the theory that we were going to bring along some famous rock stars to do a tune with Buddy. I was very naive. That didn't cut it at all. Nobody blinked."*

That same year, Chess Records, which by then belonged to MCA Corporation, released *Buddy Guy Chess Masters,* which included such classics as "First Time I Met the Blues," "Stone Crazy" and "Let Me Love You, Baby."

Stevie Ray Vaughan released *Couldn't Stand the Weather* to a rave critical response in 1984. On it were Jimi Hendrix's "Voodoo Chile (Slight Return)" and the Guitar Slim classic that Buddy had first sung when he was breaking into the clubs in Chicago, "The Things (That) I Used to Do." For Alligator, Stevie produced Lonnie Mack's comeback album, *Strike Like Lightning.* The following year, Stevie's *Soul to Soul* LP went gold, and members of Suicidal Tendencies appeared as roadies in his video of "Superstition" shown on MTV. Blues was becoming "cool" again.

Marty Salzman

In a 1986 *Musician* magazine article by J.D. Considine, Eric Clapton uttered the sentence that Marty flashed around the globe: "[Buddy Guy is] by far and without a doubt the best guitar player alive." The article was entitled "Eric Clapton Is Not GOD And He Knows It." The reference was to graffiti that had appeared in London two decades earlier, haunting Clapton for years.

If that quote had dogged him, what effect would his claim about Buddy have on Buddy's career? Now free from heroin and deep into a successful solo career singing pop ballads, Eric Clapton was considered a rock legend. If he was God, what did that make Buddy Guy?

An unsigned bluesman still playing the club circuit.

The independent blues labels were pleading for a record, but Marty and Buddy were sure they could sign with a major label and get wider exposure. But one by one, the opportunities evaporated as the major labels declined.

It began to look as if Buddy Guy had missed his opportunity to exploit his unique style. In 1958, when he first started to employ feedback into his sound, Willie Dixon dismissed Buddy for not being able to keep time. In 1965, Leonard Chess was experimenting with him as a Rhythm-and-Blues/soul artist while Clapton and the Stones were creating a rock sound influenced in large part by Buddy's stunning guitar work and powerful explosions of sound.

The new generation of blues artists were 10-20 years Buddy's junior. They regarded Buddy Guy with the same reverence that Buddy had for Muddy Waters and B.B. King. But reverence had little to do with Buddy's thrilling stage presence. Here was young blood trapped inside a middle-aged man.

Neither Buddy nor Marty wanted to sell Buddy's experience short. He would not sign with Alligator, Rounder or any of the other small blues labels that were recording many of the blues guitarists of his generation.

MARTY SALZMAN: *"We felt the type of distribution from a blues label would categorize and put this record in the blues stacks in the back of the store with minimal real AOR [album-oriented radio] or rock-type distribution. And we thought Buddy Guy with his playing could get a real distribution, a real promotion that would hopefully traverse the line between blues and pop or rock and mainstream airplay recognition."*

Likewise, any deal with a major label had to be comfortable financially. Buddy had spent a career waiting for royalty checks that either never came or were not for the promised amount. "The reason Buddy won't sign with a minor," Dick Waterman would say years after his professional association with Buddy had ended, "is because they won't give him the money up front, and he doesn't trust a computer 100 miles away to give him fair royalties."

Then there was the question of artistic freedom. Buddy's style was not simply defined. He could cross the line between raw, wailing guitar lines and soothing vocal magic in a flash. His stage shows incorporated hard rock, soul, jazz and Rhythm-and-Blues. And nothing ever sounded exactly the same twice. Whoever signed him would have to deal with a multi-faceted dynamo whose best work came fast and rode on the moods of the moment.

MARTY SALZMAN: *"We either sent letters or spoke by phone to everyone from Island to Atlantic. Some of it was done through mutual acquaintances. Somebody would say, 'Hey, I know someone at Island or somewhere else.' They'd come back, 'No, not interested.' When Stevie Ray Vaughan was taking off at CBS, I thought that was a good time to talk to them. Stevie himself had tried to persuade CBS that Buddy should be signed. If Stevie was doing so well, how about his mentor? They were not interested.*

"Atlantic expressed interest. When we played Stephen Stills' wedding, Ahmet Ertegun was there and threw his arms around Buddy. 'How are you? It's good to see you again.' He had shown a lot of interest in Buddy then and earlier years as well. Then his nephew, an A&R [artist and repertoire] guy and the person we really had to convince, came to see Buddy at the Lone Star Cafe in New York one night. After that show, I thought he looked convinced, but that just sort of evaporated into nothingness as well."

*Carlos Santana says
Buddy 'sits on the Mount
Olympus of blues.'*

In 1989, Stevie Ray Vaughan released his most critically acclaimed record to date, *In Step*. Included was Buddy's "Leave My Little Girl Alone" and "Let Me Love You, Baby," a Willie Dixon number Buddy had recorded for Chess.

Stevie Ray Vaughan

STEVIE RAY VAUGHAN: *"We've sat in with each other and done some shows together. It's always a kick. There's something about him that makes me want to (Vaughan grabs the air and bites down on a phantom object). Then Buddy Guy starts singing, and it's all over. What are you gonna do after he sings? He's neat. What he does is just raw. I don't mean at all without finesse or anything. I mean raw like raw can be real gentle. And it can be bare wires.*

"I'm trying to learn about finesse, about raw, what it can be, what it is. Just raw emotion. That's what I try to learn from Buddy. I try to learn honesty when I play. I don't know. There's something I see in Buddy. It's open honesty, and not making your move too soon. But sometimes when I get around Buddy, the only thing I know to do is just floor it. He's standing here waiting, going, 'OK, now sing!'"

Eric Clapton still was performing often with Buddy. Carlos Santana counted him as a close friend; Carlos had said Buddy Guy "is the ambassador of the blues." As helpful as these relationships were to Buddy's renewed career, the elusive major label contract still seemed out of reach. Still, there was a definite buzz in the air about Buddy.

BUDDY GUY: *"Sure, I probably could have gone to Eric or some of my friends if I didn't have the money and say, 'I'm gonna put an album out myself and do as well as be treated by some of these companies that would have me do the same thing.' So my decision was, 'Just keep playing, Buddy. Somebody will hear you, and sooner or later, you'll get an album out.' And that's why I'm saying, better late than never. And I figured something would happen to me. I just played the waiting game. I stuck with my friends and I played. And I played. I stopped worrying about the record companies."*

It disturbed Marty to know that he managed one of the 10 hottest guitarists in the world and that the other nine were all millionaires.

17 Legends

"I must have been put here for a reason. Ain't nobody ever taught me nothing. There wasn't nobody to teach me nothing. So my talent got to be God-gifted, 99$^{1}/_{2}$ percent. The rest of the stuff I watched, looked and learned."

—Buddy Guy

Marty Salzman's policy was to increase Buddy's visibility not only through Buddy's association with famous rock guitarists, but by increasing Buddy's touring schedule from an average of 30 dates a year in 1981 to more than 200 by 1989. Buddy had sold the Checkerboard in 1985 to concentrate on his touring schedule. But by 1989, he was ready to jump back into the club business because he missed having a place where he could play with his friends.

On June 9, 1989, Buddy headlined the Chicago Blues Festival. In front of more than 30,000 people, in a show broadcast across America on National Public Radio, he invited Willie Dixon on stage to sing "Little Red Rooster." He then announced that he'd just gotten his liquor license and that Legends would be open after the concert. By 10 p.m., the large, antiseptic new club at 754 Wabash Avenue—within blocks of the Loop—was open and packed with Blues Fest fans. Buddy christened the joint by playing two long sets before the 2 a.m. closing.

Longtime Elton John lyricist Bernie Taupin (pointing) visits Buddy at Legends.

BUDDY GUY: *"When I first got to Chicago, there were so many places for some-one to play. And a lot of that's gone now. So I owe this back to Chicago and the young people who are playing this now. You come in there now and I have this young kid or whoever on the stage and you say, 'Who is that?' If I don't have that club, what's he going to do? You play your way through nightclubs. The blues clubs is like the blues musicians. There's only a few of us left."*

Buddy was largely inspired by Antone's, where he had played a few times in, of all places, Austin, Texas.

BUDDY GUY: *"Clifford Antone should be like B.B. King's name should be on gui-tar, because he brought the blues to Austin. Other music was there, but he was one of those guys whose name should go down in history for what he did for blues in Austin. He brought people like Muddy Waters and Howlin' Wolf, Jimmy Reed, T-Bone Walker, everybody who the young white generation in the '60s and '70s didn't know anything about. Then up steps Stevie and the Thunderbirds, and they were liv-ing there, and he started bringing the Muddys, myself, the Juniors, whoever was left living, down there in his place. He brought the black blues to Texas. It took me a long time to go to Texas. I don't know how long it took Muddy to go there in the white market. But he played there at Antone's."*

Within a year, the roster of guests who had dropped in to listen and jam at Legends included Stevie Ray Vaughan, David Bowie, Adrian Belew, Joe Perry, Roger Daltrey, Belinda Carlisle, Sinead O'Connor, Kim Wilson and Jimmie Vaughan of the Fabulous Thunderbirds and Ron Wood and Bill Wyman of the Rolling Stones. The crowds were usually loud and large.

And, of course, it was always a thrill for Buddy to play at other venues, particularly in England. In 1990, he jumped at the chance to join Clapton at London's Royal Albert Hall, where Clapton set a Guinness Book World Record with 18 consecutive sold-out shows. There were actually three distinct show formats during the run: big-band, Clapton's own touring band, and superstar blues jams, which were held over the last three nights. Included in the blues lineup were Buddy Guy and Robert Cray.

ERIC CLAPTON: *"With Robert Cray, I knew we could rehearse and, once we got it, it would stay that way. And it would probably stay that way with me, too. I may take an extra solo. With Buddy, you didn't know what was going to happen. And that's what I wanted."*

The first blues show in London consisted mainly of old standards.

BUDDY GUY: *"The media came out the next morning. One headline said, 'This is as close to heaven as you can get.' One of them said, 'Eric played his beautiful smooth stuff, Robert played his and Buddy played a little speed.'*

"I do play blues in a speedy way now and I ring the strings, but somehow or other I just speed up sometimes to try and let people know that maybe if I had to, I could play a kind of swing blues like T-Bone Walker used to do with the big bands."

Clapton was not as pleased. He felt Buddy's performance had been affected by his drinking. True, he couldn't say with any assurance that it had been a less-than-stellar showing by his friend, but he was annoyed that Buddy's long set had not gone according to plan. The show went 75 minutes longer than the planned 90-minute set, resulting in a fine assessed on Clapton by the hall management.

Jerry Portnoy, Albert Collins, Robert Cray, Jimmie Vaughan and Eric Clapton at Royal Albert Hall, 1991.

ERIC CLAPTON: *"Buddy likes to drink. That, I thought, might be a problem because I'm referring to my own experience with alcohol. If I go on drunk, I'm going to make a mess with it and often did most of the time. So I projected my relationship with alcohol on Buddy, and I thought, 'I gotta try and keep him sober!' And the first night, we failed miserably at this.*

"I think he downed all of a bottle of brandy in a short space of time before we went on. He went on, and it was sensational. We in the band didn't know half of what was going on next. But we went along with it, and it was fantastic. Sometimes he was doing things like he'd stop the song, and he'd call me over to the microphone. 'What the fuck is he gonna do? What am I gonna do?' It was going to be one of those 'Let's-make-up-a-song-talking-about-one-another' or another one of those. He didn't actually do anything that made me feel bad even though he was nine sheets to the wind gone, but he still exercised good taste and didn't get me on the spot other than calling me to the microphone. Then, when I got there, he just wanted my company at the microphone as kind of a backup celebrity or something. So, I was off the hook. But for a minute there, I was scared shitless, and I didn't know what was gonna happen.

"Going from there, a bit later in the show he found himself out in the stalls of Albert Hall. And he was out there in the crowd. And I swear, he didn't know he was there. He kept looking around kind of like, 'What am I doing?'

"That was like, well, it's great, but it's kind of loose."

Robert Cray, on the other hand, was totally impressed.

ROBERT CRAY: *"Buddy stole the show, of course. It's like the other two of us were the students of Buddy Guy. So, Buddy just took over.*

"The show was late because of Buddy, but it was just because he would do the songs that he was gonna do. We'd get a nice blues groove going, and he'd start singing something else. That's the thing about Buddy Guy I've always appreciated. That man can go and go and go.

"You just stand back there with a smile on your face and go, 'This is Buddy Guy, man. This is the cat!' And he'll just go. We had a great time. I can remember we did a song called 'There Is Something on Your Mind,' an old R&B tune. I mean just out of nowhere. It just felt right, so we slipped right into it. We didn't rehearse it. We just did it. He'd just call the key, and we'd go right into it. That was just wonderful."

The second night of the three, Buddy, near-sober, kept looking at his watch and came in a half-hour early.

ERIC CLAPTON: *"The next night I deliberately gave him a hard time about the booze before he went on. 'Maybe you should try and cool it, you know? Just see how it goes.'*

"And then he was still trying to make crafty inroads. So, we hid it from him. We gave him a ration and then hid the fucking bottle. And he went on almost completely cold sober. It was a completely different show.

"The second night was just like scripted. And Buddy said to me, 'Well, was that better?' And the truth was, it wasn't. Before the last number, he was actually looking at his watch and saying, 'What do you think? We're doing all right, aren't we?' I said, 'You're looking at your watch on stage.'

"So cold! And the night before was so different. I said, 'What do I do here,' 'cause I'm kind of anti-booze 'cause I think it's gonna kill anyone who does it too much, but at the same time, you could see he was having a much better time. So, I didn't know what to do. I mean, I just gave up and let him do whatever."

Andrew Lauder, who in 1965 had been a wide-eyed new arrival to London's blues scene and was wowed by Buddy's first show, attended one of Clapton's 1990 blues shows. He was now president of Silvertone Records,

and he had been asked to attend the Albert Hall shows by Mike Kappas, manager of Robert Cray and John Lee Hooker. Kappas had suggested to Marty Salzman that Silvertone would be a good label for Buddy.

After seeing Buddy, Lauder told Kappas he'd like to talk to Marty about having Buddy record for his label. Marty was finally getting some interest from Virgin Records, another London-based major label that was starting a blues subsidiary called Point Blank. All of a sudden, two major labels were vying for the services of a man who hadn't recorded for a major label in nearly 20 years.

All the makings of a new surge in Buddy's popularity were even more enhanced on June 3, 1990, when Buddy presented Eric Clapton with the "Living Legend Award" on ABC Television's *International Rock Awards* program. The show was beamed around the world to an audience of more than 70 million people. Clapton scoffed in rehearsals that Buddy, of all people, should be presenting the award to him. It was Buddy, after all, whom Clapton had always placed on a pedastel. "That's poetic justice, isn't it?" Clapton said with a shrug.

After receiving the award, Clapton put down the miniature Elvis statue and began playing "Sweet Home Chicago" with a band that included Buddy, Bo Diddley, Lou Reed, Steve Tyler and Joe Perry of Aerosmith, members of Clapton's band, Neil Schon of Bad English, Sam Kinison on guitar, Richie Sambora of Bon Jovi, Billy Joel, Gary Busey and Dave Stewart of the Eurythmics.

There in a clutter on stage was a latter-day version of rock's pantheon. Bo Diddley had invented the beat. Buddy was the taproot to the real blues. Perry and Tyler had redefined the relationship between blues and rock in the 1970s. Lou Reed, looking nervous behind his dark glasses, cemented the connection between psychedelic rock and punk. Schon, with Journey, linked psychedelia with the pop hard rock sound of the late 1970s. Dave Stewart had lent legitimacy to electronic hard rock. Richie Sambora of Bon Jovi represented the new breed of superstar guitarists.

All watched Buddy for cues.

At the International Rock Awards.

*Albert Collins with
Buddy at Antone's.*

ERIC CLAPTON: *"Buddy was reading that band, watching everyone else and listening to everybody. Not very many musicians of that caliber do that. Maybe a guy will go in nervous about his popularity or his ego. He's really nervous about how he comes across. Most people of any elevated stature or fame will be concerned about themselves, making sure everything is good and presentable. Everyone else is a threat. So, if there's someone else there that's better, you've got to find a way to work it out so you can be different. It just involves a whole lot of political moves, musical moves. You can live with one another and still keep your identity.*

"Buddy didn't give a shit about any of that. He was just there, and he was listening to everybody with no concern for his own well-being. There was no one there that was a threat to him whatsoever. That kind of in-built confidence is what gives him the ability to play to any crowd. I couldn't do that, because I'd think, 'Well, I can't do this. I can't play to this crowd. They're too—something or other. I can't go with it.' Why? Because obviously I'm not to that level yet that Buddy's at. Not many people are. There's no such word as can't with Buddy."

18 The Sky Is Crying

"Within 15 minutes, I saw the highway and all the traffic. I looked at my bass player and neither one of us said a word until we landed, including Eric. I then said, 'Thanks be we're out of that.' When something's gonna happen, I guess it's gonna happen anyway."

—Buddy Guy

Buddy wasn't getting to spend much more time at Legends than he had at the Checkerboard, but big crowds on weekends when Buddy was in town were the norm. On those occasions, there was always a chance that special guests might drop by. Sunday, August 26, 1990, promised to be just such a day. B.B. King and Bobby Blue Bland were playing Chicago's famed Regal Theater. Carlos Santana was performing at a new arena just outside of Chicago. Two hours away in East Troy, Wisconsin, Eric Clapton, Stevie Ray Vaughan and Robert Cray were teaming up for the second night of a triple-header at Alpine Valley.

Marty decided he'd drive to the Santana concert and see if he could get Carlos to come back to the club. Buddy had been invited to brunch at the Four Seasons with Clapton, and the two were to proceed to Alpine Valley via helicopter. Buddy invited his bass player, Greg Rzab, to come along. Greg had been with Buddy since 1986.

Shortly after the helicopters took off, the one Rzab was flying in had to come back and land. There was a problem with the generator, and it was replaced with another. Buddy was nervous. He didn't like to fly anyway, and something like this just worried him more. During the half-hour ride to the concert site, Clapton and Buddy talked about old times.

*Stevie Ray Vaughan with
Buddy at Antone's, 1982.*

BUDDY GUY: *"Eric confessed to me on the chopper how high he was when he made the [Atlantic] album.*

"'I never told you this. I hardly remember recording with you.'

"'What the hell are you talking about?'

"'Buddy, I never told you I was into that thing. I was completely spaced. I don't know what you played.'

"I said, 'If that stuff makes you feel like that, I'm sure glad you don't mess with it anymore.'"

Both Buddy and Clapton were anxious to perform with Stevie Ray Vaughan. His new *In Step* album was being called his best ever, and his playing packed a punch that contrasted dramatically with his softer playing. Stevie didn't disappoint that day at Alpine Valley. He knew Buddy was in the audience.

STEVIE RAY VAUGHAN: *"He brings me back home. You get to play in places like this a lot. Lots of times, it seems as if so many people are gonna tell you how much they liked it without listening. It's easy to get off into just going through the motions. I try not to do that, but I catch myself. I'll go see somebody like him, and I'll realize where I've been for a while. It's drifting somewhere. There'll be nights that have the kind of emotion I really want to put into it. But to come back in and see somebody like Buddy or Otis Rush, it's like they shake you. All they have to do is look at you. You hear somebody, and it shakes your soul."*

Early in his set, Stevie followed "Tightrope" with "The Things (That) I Used to Do." Then, he lit into "Let Me Love You Baby," the song Buddy had written with Willie Dixon on his second Chess studio session in December 1960.

ROBERT CRAY: *"I can remember at one point I was backstage, and I heard a Buddy Guy song. It started up, and I ran up to the stage because I thought Buddy had joined Stevie on stage. But Stevie was singing a Buddy Guy song. And I walked up to see a big old smile on Buddy's face and Stevie looking at him [at the side of the stage] and saying, 'This is great,' and watching the reactions of the young kids grooving to a Buddy Guy song. I thought Buddy was on stage, and I wish that he had been, but he wasn't there yet."*

Stevie did a third Buddy Guy favorite in a row with "Let Me Love You Baby" and continued through a set that climaxed with Jimi Hendrix's "Voodoo Chile."

GREG RZAB: *"I remember Stevie finishing his set and walking off the stage and the applause. Everyone had their lighters and matches lit. And the applause was moving. It was thunderous. It was like, 'Stevie, check this out. You did good. These people dig your ass.'*

"It was cool to see that 'cause he'd been through a lot of things and struggled for a long time. And he was there, man. He did real good. You could see him getting better right before your eyes. It was like, look at this guy."

After Clapton's set, Stevie, Robert Cray and Buddy joined him and his band for an encore of "Sweet Home Chicago." Wild guitar runs were flying through the outdoor arena with more than 40,000 grooving to the dueling strings.

ROBERT CRAY: *"I just moved over to one side, and I was just gonna play rhythm. I took a look at everybody grabbing Stratocasters off the racks. So, I went and grabbed a steel-bodied Telecaster that I use sometimes, and I was gonna play a nice little rhythm and stay out of the way. There were too many guitar players on stage. There was Stevie Ray Vaughan. There was Eric. There was Phil who plays guitar with Eric and there was Buddy and then myself. I knew it was gonna be kind of mumbo jumbo. So I just sat off to one side and watched everybody go at it. Eric gave me a solo, too. I was so far to one side of the stage that it was hard to hear what was going on, especially with all the rhythms and solos going on. I just watched and had a good time."*

Backstage, the feeling was one of ecstasy.

GREG RZAB: *"They said, 'Man, this feels so good, we ought to take this on the road.' They were joking about it, but it was almost realistic in a way 'cause they were like, 'Wow, that would be great. We just do a Buddy Guy, Eric Clapton, Stevie Ray Vaughan tour. You know, take it on the road so everybody can feel their shit.' And Eric goes, 'Well, you know, I got Buddy coming over to Albert Hall. I would love to have you over here to play.' And Stevie, without hesitation, said, 'Yup, no problem. I'm sure I don't have anything going on, and if I do, I'll rearrange it. I'll be there.'*

"Then Buddy goes, 'Well, you know, I'd like to have you guys come down to the club tomorrow night to jam.'"

The fog was so thick after the concert that Rzab couldn't see anything beyond the green light on the dashboard of the helicopter. He looked at Buddy and said, "How the hell do these things fly in conditions like this? Should we be doing this?"

Buddy's only comfort was that helicopters fly straight up and are not likely to crash into the side of a mountain the way a plane might. When they moved Greg onto the same helicopter as Buddy and Clapton, he rationalized to himself, "Well, I'm safe because right in front of my face there's Eric Clapton and Buddy Guy, and the good Lord isn't gonna let anything happen to this 'copter, so just relax 'cause these cats are here."

As Rzab got into the waiting limousine after landing in Chicago, he looked out the back window through the dark mist and saw the fourth limousine waiting alone for the next helicopter, which was carrying Stevie and members of Clapton's entourage.

At 7 a.m. the next morning, the wreckage of the Bell 206 jet helicopter was found. It had slammed into a 100-foot ski hill next to the concert facility. It was noon before local Chicago radio stations confirmed that Stevie Ray Vaughan had been killed along with Clapton bodyguard Nigel Browne, assistant tour manager Colin Smythe, agency representative Bobby Brooks and pilot Jeff Brown.

Buddy was devastated.

People magazine would later quote Buddy as saying of Stevie Ray: "He had a skeleton key and opened doors that had been closed on us. He said, 'Let's show 'em how blues are supposed to be played.'"

BUDDY GUY: *"I think Stevie stands on top with anybody who ever picked up a guitar. He was just that good. He made me feel worse that last night 'cause he played such a tremendous set. I couldn't believe it. The guy just went two hours. Some people between songs will stop [playing] just to figure out what goes next. He just goes one to another and just plays his heart out."*

ERIC CLAPTON: *"Right after [Stevie Ray Vaughan's death], I started to play a lot more. I felt all the guitar players in the world suddenly had a lot more to do out of the night.*

"First of all, there was this massive meeting between not just the musicians but the road crew. We had a day off, and we sat in Chicago and over the phone I spoke to the production chief of the crew, and he had all the crew in one room. We had all the musicians in another room. And we kind of argued about whether we should quit and go home or go on. I mean, we lost Stevie Ray, but we also lost Nigel and Colin from our outfit. And the boys in the crew were very protective about those two.

"I think, first of all, they may have thought I was only considering the loss of this great musician. I had to make them realize that I was sensitive to their feelings about the loss of our two boys as well. It took a while. It took about an hour of discussion on the phone to really get a unanimous vote on carrying on. We had five more shows to do. First of all, some people were saying we want to grieve in private. And I offered the option that if we all went home, then it would be a lot sadder. It would be a lot more difficult to bear if all of us packed up our bags and went back to our various homes. We'd feel rotten once we got there. After a while, there was a massive agreement on that. So we went on to St. Louis.

*Buddy always carries
memories of Stevie Ray
Vaughan with him.*

"That first night was very very difficult to play, to keep my mind clear. I was distracted by visions of the people we had lost. It got better day by day, but it seemed to me I had to play a lot more. And then in the encore, I'd come on and play improvised blues solos out of the blue. And it seemed that was the thing to do like a side tribute to Stevie Ray. I'm consciously approaching my playing with him in mind these days."

19 Harvest

"My mom told me, 'You know, if you don't want to leave this earth, don't come.' She said, 'Son, don't bring me no flowers when I'm dead. Bring 'em now, so I can smell 'em.'"

—Buddy Guy

After 32 years in the business, a wisened and weathered Buddy Guy had a list of as many things he didn't want from a record company as things he did want. Now, in 1990, he was able to choose between two labels, Silvertone and Virgin. Of primary importance were selection of material and style of play. He also didn't want to record on a label that was strictly blues. Nor did he want a record like John Lee Hooker's *The Healer*, where there could be a danger of being eclipsed by guest stars. That didn't mean, of course, that he didn't want his big-name musical friends to sit in with him.

BUDDY GUY: *"If they call it selling out because I'm joining the rock people who are famous and playing, I call it dying out if I don't because without Stevie, Eric and them, I doubt I would be heard as much as I'm heard now. Them guys have done so much for black people, not only me, but when Muddy was living, they lifted him, Howlin' Wolf, everybody. So, I don't give a shit what anybody says about that."*

The first thing Virgin asked was what material Buddy would be recording. The label had signed Albert Collins and Johnny Winter, and was looking for a whole roster of blues artists. Silvertone's Andrew Lauder seemed to be more interested in Buddy as a person than as a commodity. Lauder scored points with Buddy when he didn't ask him what material he would be recording. Lauder and his associate, Michael Tedesco, not only loved Buddy's performing style, but they felt that, unlike an Albert Collins who had many albums on the market, Buddy was a legend without much product to back it up. There was a potentially eager market waiting for a new Buddy Guy album.

Buddy went with Silvertone.

MICHAEL TEDESCO: *"Obviously, we knew of his influence on a lot of people. It was always, 'Gee, it would be great if these guys want to show up and be on the*

record, but if they didn't show up and play on the record, it would still be a great Buddy Guy record.' That was the first and foremost issue. The fact that great musicians like Clapton, Knopfler and Richie Hayward are on it is definitely an asset to us. And we're grateful and thrilled they're on there. But at the end of the day, people aren't going to listen to this record and go, 'God, what a great Clapton or Knopfler track.' They're going to go, 'This guy Buddy is the real thing.'"

The anxiety level over recording his first significant album in 10 years was enormous. In the blues world, his contemporaries uniformly agreed that he deserved more recognition than he got. But would a bluesman who was considered revolutionary in 1965 still be relevant 25 years later? Then there were those who felt he was stuck in a rut, milking his old material and ignoring the best of the songs he'd written while still at Chess. Blues purists like John Hammond and Jerry Portnoy felt he was selling out by trying too hard to identify with rock music at the expense of his roots.

JOHN HAMMOND: *"My gut feeling is he wants to make it big like Jimi Hendrix, like Stevie Ray Vaughan, and somehow he just can't. Instead of sticking to that incredible power he has in blues music, he tries to bridge the gap and get into a wider audience and whiter audience. And I feel he doesn't have to. He could have been less successful and better as a blues artist. I've been on so many shows where Buddy and Junior get up there, and it's a parody of blues. It really makes me sick, and yet I've seen them on another night and gotten that old feeling [when] they play a set that's just magnificent. That's rarer and rarer. I think Buddy's great strength is in his ability to play blues his own way. And when you start to compromise that or alter it to suit an audience, then you diminish your power and your strength.*
"I just know how great Buddy is, and how good he could be, and the fact he doesn't play blues every night is staggering to me."

JERRY PORTNOY: *"Buddy is one of the absolute greatest at breaking that band down and playing quiet and really teasing, teasing that guitar, which I really love— playing real soft and teasing the notes out and, you know, he's got a beautiful touch on the guitar. But a lot of times he gets into this Hendrix thing or whatever that he seems to like doing, too. And if that's what floats your boat, that's cool, but a lot of people like to hear him just settle down and really play."*

Of course, Silvertone certainly didn't want to ignore Buddy's commercial potential.

ANDREW LAUDER: *"We want to do a lot of records with Buddy Guy. I don't think we want to put him in a blues pigeonhole. There can be lots more people if they get a chance to hear it. That's what we found out with Robert Cray. Even John Lee Hooker's album is a blues album for people who didn't think they like blues. If you listen to Mark Knopfler, you can appreciate Robert Cray. Why not Buddy Guy if you listen to Stevie Ray Vaughan? There's enough sales out there to justify making the effort. And I think he didn't want to be on the Alligators or Rounders."*

MARTY SALZMAN: *"I didn't want him to do any of the old stuff that just sounded like rehashed Buddy Guy. On the other hand, I didn't want him to be Buddy Guy, rock star. Buddy's a bluesman, and I didn't want to see him try to be too hip and get away from what makes Buddy Guy Buddy Guy."*

There would be no excuses for a poor recording this time. Silvertone allowed him at least two weeks in the studio, much longer than any other recording session he'd ever had. The sessions, produced by Buddy fan and frequent Roxy Music bass player John Porter, took place at Battery Studios in London, a modern 24-track facility with overdubbing capabilities. Buddy handled the recording sessions the same way he handles every gig, jumping in with both feet and without a set list.

Greg Rzab was on bass guitar. Mick Weaver, from Joe Cocker's Grease Band, was on keyboards. Neil Hubbard, another one-time Roxy Music band member, backed up Buddy's guitar. Richie Hayward of Little Feat played drums.

JOHN PORTER: *"When I first heard Buddy, you thought his head was gonna explode when he started singing, and he always felt that anything was possible with his guitar playing. It could go off in any direction. It was explosive, real fire. B.B. King is a wonderful player. Otis Rush, wonderful. Freddy King—all wonderful players, but none quite had the fire Buddy had and still has. You can always recognize Buddy when he was on those Chess sessions. You could always pick him out. If he was playing a solo, you knew straight away it was him. I just love him and feel so close to him."*

Rehearsals started smoothly in London, in January 1991. On the third day, Buddy told the band to play in C, ran through half a tune and then told Porter, 'OK, let's do it,' and the tapes were rolling. To Buddy, two weeks was an unbelievable gift of time. To Porter it was a crunch.

JOHN PORTER: *"We only had the band for six days. I think, God, if we'd had them for two weeks, it would have been unbelievable, but it is what it is."*

In one week, they had the rhythm tracks down for more than a dozen tunes, including scratch vocals by Buddy, many of which stayed on the finished cuts. They were that good.

The second week of the studio sessions, female singers and a horn section were brought in to add their parts. Buddy was inspired to be working with such good musicians.

BUDDY GUY: *"Working with these guys was almost like walking into a Baptist church. When you go in, you can tell as soon as the preacher opens his mouth or sings some good songs or has a good prayer, and you just be sitting there listening to him. It was like when Martin Luther King used to speak, no matter what he said, it was how he said it. It's the same with a good drummer, guitar player and piano player. These guys came in and made me feel, 'Buddy, shit! Kick yourself in the butt. You gotta get out. If you don't get it out now, you don't have it.'"*

Near the end of the sessions, Jeff Beck came to the studios to add his licks to "Mustang Sally" and "Early in the Morning." Greg Rzab was struck by Beck's work on "Mustang Sally."

GREG RZAB: *"Man, he played this chordal thing. Wherever it was coming from, he overdubbed that part on there, and I was sitting there watching him do this. You could see all the muscles and everything just tensed up. He'd slam his foot down,*

*With Jeff Beck during
Damn Right sessions.*

and the veins were popping out of his arms, and it was just like intensity, man. It was really inspiring. It just flowed through him. It was just so intense."

When Beck was finished, he and Buddy went to another room at the studio and they played together for a while.

BUDDY GUY: *"I don't know what he got, but he stopped me and had me sitting with my mouth wide open. I said, 'Man, what the hell you doing?' And then Porter told us to take two acoustics into the room and let him turn the mike on. Something might come of it. I just sat there and played some Muddy Waters licks with him, and he played slide."*

Those impromptu acoustic sessions remain unreleased.

After the recording sessions, Porter took the tracks to a studio in Ireland where Eric Clapton added his guitar to "Early in the Morning" and "Mustang Sally." Clapton couldn't make the studio sessions because he was both recording and facing a tax deadline in Dublin.

ERIC CLAPTON: *"We were short on time because I was in rehearsals in Dublin, and John Porter brought the tapes with him. He'd already decided what tapes I should play on. Those two songs were singled out for me to overdub. I didn't really have the time to do much more. So, we actually did it quite quickly, in three or four hours.*

"I just played as if it were a session. I didn't think about it being Buddy, really. I played it as if I was playing for anybody's album. And I played the way I play."

BUDDY GUY: *"I just left it with him. Wherever they figured he would fit in. He's got pretty good taste for what he wants to do anyway. To somebody of his caliber I wouldn't say, 'Eric, play this!' I just let him listen to all the stuff, and if he feels like* *he can put some Eric Clapton in there, I would appreciate whatever he does. I can understand his obligations. He didn't refuse to play. He said, 'Bring the tapes up here.' I'm sure it's worth sending the tapes up to Dublin to him so it can save him $20 million."*

Porter ultimately didn't use Clapton's track on "Mustang Sally."

Not everybody liked the idea that Buddy was recording "Mustang Sally" in the first place. And certainly, Buddy's fans could not be pleased with the final result—even though it became Buddy's first single in more than 20 years—because of this bitter irony: The cut didn't include a single note from Buddy's own guitar. Beck would, in fact, return to the studio to recut portions of his sizzling guitar run.

BRUCE IGLAUER: *"If Buddy had said to me, let's do a new version of 'Mustang Sally,' I'd have roared—not with approval. It's a trite song. You put Buddy with a really well-written lyric that hasn't been done to death, and he'll get something out of it. I think the reason people should make records is not because the song is apropos of their background, but because it's an exciting performance that speaks to today's audience."*

John Hiatt's "Where Is The Next One Coming From" was the most pop-oriented song recorded. Buddy's teenage daughter, Rashawnna—one of Buddy's two children with his second wife, Jennifer—had picked the Hiatt song out of several Buddy had been listening to in the car when he took her to school. Buddy happened to identify with the message about an alcoholic whose only concern is getting his next drink.

BUDDY GUY: *"You almost have to sympathize with a musician who has a drinking or drug problem. I can play guitar now and they'll make you drink before they'll feed you. You just play, and I don't have to worry where the next one is coming from. [I can remember when] I wanted to know where the next dollar was coming from so I could catch the bus that goes to the next joint where someone would see me and say, 'You know where the next one is coming from because I'm gonna hire you.' So, I don't condone or condemn these guys for not being strong. This ain't an easy life."*

There were three new Buddy Guy songs: The title cut, "Too Broke to Spend the Night" and "Rememberin' Stevie," an eerie instrumental that was recorded in darkness. As Buddy played, he flashed back to that night at Alpine Valley when things had started so beautifully and had ended so horribly.

BUDDY GUY: *"Stevie walked up to me backstage that night at Alpine Valley. Eric was playing something, and I was sitting over in the corner by myself. Stevie came over and said, 'Hear that there? Hear that there?' He said, 'You do that to me every time I see you.'*

"I said, 'Well, man, you just did me.'

"He looked over at me and said, 'Get out of here!' And we started laughing and joking about it. He said, 'Just wait 'til we get back out there, man. We gotta go out. We gotta go out. We gotta play something together.'

"I said, 'Well, I've been waiting for that.'

Backstage at the Beacon,
New York City, 1989.

"He said, 'We gonna get a record out, and we're gonna do something together.'

"It was like this guy was with me in the studio. Every time I got ready to sing, I'd go off into this little room. They came to me once and said, 'I thought you were tired. You go lock up by yourself.'

"I said, 'No, I'm just remembering Stevie.' They all looked at me and just sat there. Nobody said nothing. Then, they turned down the lights and said, 'Let him go.' And I said to myself, 'That's exactly what I want to do.' Let me have my fun dedicating this to him because if there's a heaven up there, they got a band up there and one day I'm gonna play with it. It's the best band you ever heard: Otis Spann, Fred Below, Muddy Waters, Stevie Ray Vaughan with Little Walter on the harmonica. What a band!"

Buddy returned to England a month later, again as Clapton's guest for six Royal Albert Hall concerts. Also in the lineup were Albert Collins and Jimmie Vaughan on guitar, Jamie Oldaker on drums, Jerry Portnoy on harmonica, Johnny Johnson on keyboards, Chuck Leavell on keyboards and Joey

*All-Star lineup at Royal
Albert Hall, 1991:
Jerry Portnoy, Albert
Collins, Robert Cray,
Jimmie Vaughan, Buddy
and Joey Spampinato.*

Spampinato on bass. The six shows were Jimmie Vaughan's first time on stage
since playing with his brother at Alpine Valley.

JIMMIE VAUGHAN: *"These were the same guys I played with the last time that
I played. This was sort of a healing thing for me. I didn't want to play. It was such
a shock. We're all just trying—I mean, how do you get over that? I don't know how
to get over it. But I realized I'm ready to carry on with my life and get back into it.
And for me to play guitar and see these guys was an extreme. . .an extremely healing
deal, you know? At first [when Eric called], I went, 'Well, I don't know.' Then I
thought, 'This is perfect. This makes sense.' In some way that I couldn't explain, it
made sense. Any time I can play with Buddy Guy, I will. Any time I can play with
any of these guys, I will.*

Jimmie Vaughn

"One of the biggest things I learned from Buddy is you just look into yourself and let it happen. He'll give me a solo, and I'll start playing, and he'll go, 'Take your time. Take your time.' That's what it means to me. You don't have to jump out and play a bunch of shit you learned off a record copying something. Just wait! Own it! Know and go with it. That's what gives me the most satisfaction, playing what I feel."

Clapton, more than ever committed to sobriety, remained nervous about what Buddy was going to do each night.

ERIC CLAPTON: *"We probably start with 'Hoochie Coochie Man,' but how long that will go on for and what it will turn into, we have no knowledge. Everyone else is*

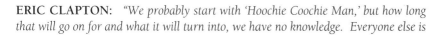

*pretty much the way it's rehearsed, which is great. It needs some kind of organiza-
tion. It can't be all Buddy, but he's got the space and the room. And he can live up
to it. If you've got the nerve to do that, fine. But you've also got to be able to entertain and make good music, too. It's a kind of license a lot of people abuse and don't
really get away with. But he can do it."*

Clapton tried to put a limit on alcohol at the shows, much to the dis-
gruntlement of Albert Collins and Buddy Guy. Whether it worked or not was
academic. The shows were coming off like clockwork, and as in the year
before, Buddy was stealing the show with the final set of four showcases after
Johnny Johnson, Albert Collins and Robert Cray.

On the final night, Clapton mistakenly introduced Buddy early while
Robert Cray walked out on the stage. When it was time for Buddy's entrance,
Clapton motioned toward the curtain in his introduction. No Buddy!

All of a sudden, the spotlights rained down in the center of the huge
amphitheater. There was Buddy dead center of the arena, wailing away on
"I'm Down."

He'd surprised Clapton again, and everyone on the stage was exulting in
Buddy's license to go over the edge.

20 The Blues Flame

"I think there's a little bit of
Buddy Guy in every song we do."

—Ron Wood

A s his schedule grew busier, Buddy often thought of his friend
Howlin' Wolf and his dogged manner in fighting death. The Wolf,
plagued by chronic kidney trouble, would book shows only in cities
with a dialysis machine. After each exhaustive treatment, he'd go
straight to his gig.

Bill Wyman liked to tell the story about the night shortly before The
Wolf died in 1976 when he walked into the Rolling Stones concert in Chicago
and got a standing ovation.

BILL WYMAN: *"Buddy took The Wolf into the audience. As they walked him out
into the audience to his seat, groups of people started to recognize him. They stood
up and applauded. Then, more stood up and applauded. And then more. There
were about 16,000 in the audience. And by the time he sat down, the whole stadium
was standing and applauding him. It was a wonderful moment. He died four
months after that."*

BUDDY GUY: *"At least I've heard these blues people play. Whether people accept
it or not, black spirituals and black blues are part of all music. You give it to me,
and I'm hoping to be around long enough to give it to somebody else. I'm hoping
somebody will say the same thing about me sooner or later. Telling about it is the
only way to keep it alive unless we're able to play it."*

*James Cotton and Buddy
at the Checkerboard
after Muddy Waters'
funeral, 1983.*

Buddy's thoughts also turned to Muddy Waters, whom he visualized slapping sense into a young, impressionable and starving bluesman in the back of that red Chevrolet station wagon, giving the youngster a salami sandwich for much-needed sustenance. Muddy died in 1983.

BUDDY GUY: *"Muddy Waters' drummer Ray Allison came to the club on 43rd Street and said, 'Old man is kinda sick. He got an irregular heartbeat.' Junior was saying, 'Hey, man, let's go see Muddy.' So, I said, 'Call him up and see if he's home.' I called him and he answered the phone. I said, 'Me and Junior are on our way out there.' I said, 'You're not doing good. You're sick.' He's nasty. He called me a motherfucker. 'Motherfucker, I ain't sick! Don't let them goddamn blues die on me, all right?' I said OK. And the next call was from the international press, that he'd*

passed away. That's why I feel strongly about it now. Every time I go to the stage, he's somewhere telling me what he was telling before he passed. 'Don't let it die!' And as long as I'm alive, I won't. I may go crazy once in a while, but I never will forget the Hoochie Coochie Man wherever I play, man. That guy is the blues.

"The year Michael Jackson won all the Grammys, they flashed Muddy Waters' picture up on national television just because he died. I say, flash my face on that Grammy while I'm alive, so I can see it instead of waiting 'til I'm dead."

In November 1990, Alligator informed Buddy that it was planning on re-releasing an old French Buddy and Junior album from the Isabell vaults. This was an acoustic LP Buddy and Junior had recorded in 1981, again in one afternoon session with improvised lyrics and spontaneous energy. It looked

like there would be two new releases coming out within two months of each other, the Alligator release in April and Silvertone in June. Buddy asked Alligator to hold its release for two months so as not to confuse buyers. Iglauer agreed and promised to call the album *Alone & Acoustic* to further distinguish it from the Silvertone album.

Damn Right, I've Got the Blues was released in late August and *Alone & Acoustic* in October. In a letter to the media that accompanied press copies of the Alligator release, Iglauer wrote: "By the way, we made a deal to release this master long before Buddy signed his new contract with Silvertone, and held the release date at his request, so this is not some quickly plotted ripoff to exploit Buddy's recent heightened visibility."

Billboard magazine listed Buddy as a "new artist" when the Silvertone CD came out. *Rolling Stone* reviewed the two releases together. Within months, MCA put out *Buddy Guy—The Complete Chess Studio Recordings*, covering all his own sessions with Chess recorded between 1960 and 1967. Following close behind that, Rhino Records re-released the Atlantic LP, *Buddy Guy & Junior Wells Play the Blues,* and a compilation called *The Very Best of Buddy Guy.* That release included the demo tape Buddy had made at WXOK in 1957, as well as selections from Chess, JSP and Blind Pig.

Buddy felt he needed a manager with more blues experience and hired Scott A. Cameron, who had managed both Muddy Waters and Willie Dixon. Cameron had also worked with more than 100 blues artists and their heirs in getting back royalties from record companies. At age 55, Buddy wanted to enjoy his success before he was too old, unlike so many of his musical heroes.

SCOTT CAMERON: *"We have always worked with innovators instead of imita-tors. That's what Buddy has always been to me, is an innovator. This has been my career, to work with innovative music instead of grabbing some great big Rock-and-Roll band that has a couple of hits and then goes off into obscurity when my bank book is pretty full.*

"I think Buddy's guitar work is innovative. I think a lot of his stage presence is innovative, and he creates his own music. He doesn't imitate somebody else's, except during his shows. Then he does a little bit of John Lee Hooker, Jimmy Reed, Stevie Ray, Muddy Waters, and others."

Buddy's visibility and popularity were finally catching up with his leg-endary status. In 1992 he walked away with five W.C. Handy Awards, the Grammy of blues. His work with Clapton at Royal Albert Hall appeared on the *24 Nights* compilation and on one song from the *Rush* film soundtrack, "Don't Know which Way to Go" by Willie Dixon. Hot country artist Travis Tritt featured a sizzling version of Buddy's "Leave My Little Girl Alone" on his million-selling *t-r-o-u-b-l-e* album.

Silvertone was pleased. It had an artist whose credentials were real and who also fraternized with contemporary rock heroes. It was just a question of selling a black 55-year-old bluesman as a hit-maker.

In February 1992, a photograph of a smiling Buddy Guy was flashed to an international television audience. He had just been awarded a Grammy Award for "Best Contemporary Blues LP." Unlike Muddy Waters, he had lived to see his image on television.

At the 1989 New Orleans Jazz Festival.

Damn Right, I've Got the Blues did not outsell John Lee Hooker's *The Healer*, but the Grammy-winning album sold in the hundreds of thousands. It was enough to get Buddy back in the studio in May 1992, with his album-by-album contract with Silvertone.

Feels Like Rain, a 1993 release, was a logical continuation of his work on *Damn Right, I've Got the Blues.* Eric Clapton and Jeff Beck were absent, but Bonnie Raitt, John Mayall and Paul Rodgers reinforced the blues/rock connections with Bonnie contributing slide guitar and background vocals on the title cut, written by John Hiatt. It had been Hiatt's "Thing Called Love" that sparked Raitt's comeback in 1989, and Buddy had enjoyed performing Hiatt's "Where Is the Next One Coming From" on his last album.

Once again John Porter produced and brought Little Feat's Richie Hayward back to drum, this time adding Little Feat's Bill Payne to share keyboard work with Marty Grebb and Ian McLagan of Rolling Stones fame. Hayward said things really clicked the second week into the session.

RICHIE HAYWARD: *"A lot of stuff happened because Buddy just broke into the song in the studio. He was standing right in the room with me singing and playing the guitar. It was almost like being there (in the audience) for a live show except I was at the drums. A couple of times I almost stopped. Then I realized, 'Oh, I gotta keep this going.' It was really great."*

Just before *Feels Like Rain* was released, Buddy bought a Rolls Royce for his wife, Jennifer, and a Ferrari for himself. He was finally feeling more confident about his career.

BUDDY GUY: *"It crosses my mind every night when I say my prayers or when I get up in the morning: How could they wait 'til I get down near 60 years old 'fore they give me a real shot at it? I guess if it was meant for me, I'd have been Chuck*

Berry or Eric Clapton or whoever. But it didn't happen. Now, I'm happy with my little success lately. I'm not at the top of the ladder, but I think somebody can see me now."

Even Buddy's own son had no idea of his father's influence when he began playing guitar in 1989.

BUDDY GUY: *"Greg, my middle child by my first wife, went wild over Prince. I got him a guitar and amp. In a week, he comes back and says, 'Dad, I got Prince.'*

"I says, 'You didn't.' I gave him a couple of bars, and he was playing it.

"He says, 'I got that down. Who should I listen to next?'

"'Maybe you should try Hendrix.'

"'Who's that?'

"I said, 'Ask for Jimi Hendrix.'

"Then he sees a clip on Hendrix on the educational channel. He called me and said, 'Daddy, I saw Hendrix. I see what you mean. Know what he said?'

"'What?'

"'He said he learned from you. I didn't know you could play like that.'

"I said, 'You never asked.'"

Discography

SOUTH SIDE BLUES JAM
(Junior Wells, Buddy Guy
and Otis Spann)
Delmark DC 628 Cassette
Delmark DD 628 CD

HOODOO MAN BLUES
(Junior Wells, Buddy Guy)
Delmark DC 612 Cassette
Delmark DD 612 CD

ALONE & ACOUSTIC
(Buddy Guy, Junior Wells)
Alligator ALC 4802 Cassette
Alligator ALCD 4802 CD

STONE CRAZY
Alligator ALC 4723 Cassette
Alligator ALCD 4723 CD

COMING AT YOU
(Buddy Guy, Junior Wells)
Vanguard 79262 Cassette
Vanguard 79262 CD

MY TIME AFTER AWHILE
Vanguard 141-42 Cassette
Vanguard 141-42 CD

HOLD THAT PLANE
Vanguard 79323 Cassette
Vanguard 79323 CD

THIS IS BUDDY GUY
Vanguard 79290 Cassette
Vanguard 79290 CD

A MAN & THE BLUES
Vanguard 79272 Cassette
Vanguard 79272 CD

**DRINKIN' TNT 'N'
SMOKIN' DYNAMITE**
Blind Pig BP 71182 Cassette
Blind Pig BP 71182 CD

PLAY THE BLUES
(Buddy Guy, Junior Wells)
Rhino R2-70299 Cassette
Rhino R2-70299 CD

**THE VERY BEST OF
BUDDY GUY**
Rhino R2-70280 Cassette
Rhino R2-70280 CD

Discography (Continued)

BUDDY & THE JUNIORS
(Buddy Guy, Junior Wells
and Junior Mance)
MCA MCAD 10517 Cassette
MCA MCAD 10517 CD

**I WAS WALKING
THROUGH THE WOODS**
MCA/Chess CH 9135 Cassette
MCA/Chess CH 9135 CD

**LEFT MY BLUES IN SAN
FRANCISCO**
MCA/Chess CH 9262 Cassette
MCA/Chess CH 31265 CD

BUDDY GUY
MCA/Chess CH 9115 Cassette
MCA/Chess CH 9115 CD

**COMPLETE CHESS
RECORDINGS**
MCA/Chess CHD1-9337 Cas.
MCA/Chess CHD1-9337 CD

**DAMN RIGHT,
I'VE GOT THE BLUES**
Silvertone 1462-2-J Cassette
Silvertone 1462-2-J CD

FEELS LIKE RAIN
Silvertone 41498 Cassette
Silvertone 41498 CD

Index

151